ACUTE ALCOHOLIC INTOXICATION

ACUTE ALCOHOLIC INTOXICATION

A CRITICAL REVIEW

By

HENRY W. NEWMAN, M.D.

STANFORD UNIVERSITY PRESS
STANFORD UNIVERSITY, CALIFORNIA

STANFORD UNIVERSITY PRESS
STANFORD UNIVERSITY, CALIFORNIA

LONDON: HUMPHREY MILFORD
OXFORD UNIVERSITY PRESS

THE BAKER AND TAYLOR COMPANY
55 FIFTH AVENUE, NEW YORK

THE MARUZEN COMPANY
TOKYO, OSAKA, KYOTO, SENDAI

PRINTED AND BOUND IN THE UNITED STATES
OF AMERICA BY STANFORD UNIVERSITY PRESS

To the

Memory

of my Teacher

HENRY GEORGE MEHRTENS

PREFACE

It is not the purpose of this book to present a digest of the voluminous literature covering the various aspects of alcohol. Rather, it has been our endeavor to present in some detail the more recent contributions to those phases of the subject with which we ourselves have worked and in regard to which we have some basis for critical judgment. This, then, is the explanation of the somewhat parochial nature of the bibliography.

The controversial nature of most of the problems considered makes a final answer in all cases impossible. We have tried to present all the pertinent data as impartially as possible, although such an attitude is difficult to maintain in regard to problems with which we have been actively engaged in the laboratory. Abundant as the work on alcohol has been, the subjects on which authorities have come to complete agreement, indicative of final solution of the problem, will be seen to be remarkably few. The primary objective of this volume is to delineate those aspects of the subject most in need of clarification, with a presentation of the factual data so far obtained. By so taking stock of our knowledge, we may gain some degree of orientation toward future approaches to the problems.

The biochemistry of alcohol has received much less attention from those best qualified for its investigation than its importance merits. Most of those engaged in alcohol research have been interested in the broader field of the effect of the substance on the human organism, with the result that the more fundamental knowledge of the economy of alcohol in the body has been relatively neglected. Recent work demonstrating the interrelationship between alcohol metabolism and carbohydrate and protein metabolism will, it is to be hoped, direct the attention of biochemists and physiologists to this problem, the importance of which lies not only in the field of research on alcohol, but on metabolism in general as well.

A particular effort has been made to present in a complete yet concise manner the data bearing on the chemical diagnosis of drunkenness, which has become of considerable medicolegal importance. We hope that the ready availability of this information may aid in the intelligent application of this procedure, as well as in the understanding of the limitations of its field of usefulness.

H. W. N.

San Francisco, California
August 15, 1941

CONTENTS

Part One. General Actions of Ethyl Alcohol

Part Two. Toxicology of Ethyl Alcohol

PART ONE

GENERAL ACTIONS OF ETHYL ALCOHOL

CHAPTER I

ABSORPTION AND DISTRIBUTION

Whether or not it is justifiable to consider alcohol as a food, its consumption represents a considerable proportion of the caloric intake of a great many individuals, while in a far greater number enough is ingested to be of importance from the metabolic as well as the pharmacologic viewpoint. The amount of alcohol in foodstuffs is negligible, the sole source being that ingested as one or other of the various alcoholic beverages. These may be roughly divided into two groups—those produced by carbohydrate fermentation alone, and those in which the alcoholic content is increased after fermentation by distillation. In the former category are found beer and ale, derived from grain, and dry wine, derived from fruit juice, notably that of the grape; while in the latter are brandy, distilled from wine, and whisky, distilled from fermented grain. Rum and gin fall in the second group, while sweet wines are intermediate, being mixtures of dry wine and brandy.

The alcoholic concentration of beer ranges from 3 to 8%, dry wine from 7 to 14%, sweet wine from 18 to 24%, and whisky, brandy, rum, and gin from 40 to 50%. Cocktails, highballs, and the myriad of mixed drinks generally do not exceed an alcoholic concentration of 20%, deriving much of their dilution from the ice used to cool them. Thus the beer and wine drinker consumes a beverage containing about 3 to 7% alcohol, while the devotee of so-called "hard liquor" ingests alcohol in a concentration of about 20%.

The amount of alcohol gaining entrance to the body other than orally is entirely insignificant. Suffice it to say that for therapeutic and experimental studies administration subcutaneously, intraperitoneally, intravenously, by rectum, and via the inspired air has on occasion been achieved.

Absorption from stomach.—After ingestion, alcohol enjoys a sojourn of greater or lesser extent in the stomach, depending on a variety of conditions. It is one of the few substances which may be absorbed directly from the stomach. Faiteberg and Medevedew (1),* using dogs with a Pawlow pouch, found that within 20 to 30 minutes after administration of 1 cc. of 40% alcohol per kilogram of body weight into the pouch the respiratory quotient fell, indicating combustion of alcohol, and alcohol could be recovered from the breath and blood. If the mucous membrane of the pouch were experimentally inflamed, the speed of absorption was diminished. Edkins and Murray (2) found alcohol to be absorbed from the isolated stomach of the cat. They used decerebrate cats, tied off the stomach at the esophagus, and inserted a cannula into the pylorus through which the alcohol could be administered. At the end of a period of one hour after the injection of 60 cc. of 5% alcohol they determined the alcohol content of the gastric contents, and found appreciable absorption to have taken place. The amount of absorption was increased by simultaneous administration of carbon dioxide.

Absorption from intestine.—Absorption from the stomach is, however, slow compared with that from other portions of the alimentary tract. Thus Higgins (3) found that after oral administration of doses of alcohol of 30 and 45 cc. in man the respiratory quotient fell in from 4 to 15 minutes—appreciably faster than in the case of the dogs with Pawlow pouches. Cori, Villiaume, and Cori (4) administered 2.5 to 5.0 cc. of 10 to 40% alcohol gastrically to fasting rats of 140 to 200 grams weight, and analyzed the gut and its contents for alcohol at intervals after administration. They found that massage of the stomach through the abdominal wall was effective in greatly increasing the speed of absorption of the alcohol, owing to expedition of emptying of the stomach into the small intestine. They concluded that the rapidity of absorption was roughly proportional to the rate of emptying of the stomach. On the other hand, Hanzlik

* See numbered bibliography at the end of the chapter.

(5), using the isolated stomach and intestinal loop technic in cats and dogs, found the rates of absorption from the stomach and the small intestine to be about equal.

Effect of concentration.—The concentration of the ingested alcohol also plays a part in the rate of absorption. Thus Miles (6) gave a dose of 0.5 cc. of alcohol per kilogram to human subjects. This was given in two forms, a concentrated form in 100 cc. of grape juice and a dilute in 1,000 cc. of grape juice. The curve of blood alcohol against time after this dose showed a slower rise with the dilute beverage, with a lower maximum concentration, indicating slower absorption. Mellanby (7) found that on oral administration to dogs 20% alcohol was absorbed more rapidly than 5%, as judged by the rate of increment of blood alcohol concentration. This was especially noticeable with large doses. Hanzlik (5), using intestinal loops, found 10% alcohol to be absorbed most rapidly, with 5% and 50% absorbed less rapidly, and 95% least rapidly. Thus evidence seems conclusive that absorption of alcohol is maximal in speed with concentrations of from 10 to 20%, lower and higher concentrations being absorbed more slowly. It is understandable that the greater bulk of the low concentrations would slow passage through the stomach, while it is more than possible that the higher concentrations are effective in depressing gastric motility and thus prolonging emptying time of the stomach. Inflammation produced by the high concentrations would also slow absorption, possibly by producing an outpouring of mucus that would render the absorbing surface less accessible to the alcohol.

Type of beverage.—The type of alcoholic beverage has its own effect on rapidity of absorption, entirely apart from the difference in concentration represented. Thus Mellanby (7) found that when he administered 50 cc. of alcohol to a dog as 28.5% whisky the blood alcohol concentration rose more rapidly and to a higher maximum than when the same amount of alcohol was administered as stout of 5.5 or 3.9% concentration. That this was not due to concentration alone was shown by administering the whisky diluted to the same strength as the stout, when the same difference in speed of absorption was manifest. It was concluded that some component present in the stout and not in the whisky was responsible for the slowing of absorption. From what we know of the importance of gastric motility on speed of absorption of alcohol, it is probable that this substance has its effect on the emptying time of the stomach; but just what it is is not known. Similar studies with a wider variety of beverages seem indicated.

Mechanism of absorption.—Once past the stomach, absorption is quite rapid. The mechanism of absorption in the case of alcohol is probably that of simple diffusion, since it passes readily through cell membranes. In fact, Hanzlik (5) found absorption from intestinal loops to proceed to a disappearance of 30% of the contents in an animal immediately after death, in which case the absorbed alcohol could not be removed by the circulating blood but must disappear solely by diffusion. Alcohol passes directly into the blood stream, and is carried off unchanged. A good conception of the rapidity of passage through the mucosa can be gained from the fact that, in spite of the rapid blood flow through the gut wall, the concentration of alcohol in the venous blood leaving a loop of small intestine containing alcohol may approach 1%, while the concentration of the arterial blood is not a fifth of that value (8).

Influence of food.—The presence of food in the stomach, taken either before or with the alcohol, is a potent factor in influencing the speed of absorption of alcohol. In this it acts in two ways. First, it greatly prolongs the emptying time of the stomach, and so delays the passage of alcohol into the small intestine where it could be rapidly absorbed. However, another factor must also operate, for it has been shown that different types of foodstuff act in different degree. Mellanby (7) found that the administration of a meal of bread and milk to dogs before the giving of alcohol had a marked effect on the blood alcohol curve, the rate of increment being reduced as well as the maximum concentration. The effect was most pronounced in the first three-hour period. Milk was found to be the potent element in the meal, as it alone was effective in producing the same effect. Skimmed milk was also effective, but in lesser degree; so it was concluded that milk fat was an important factor. Suet, however, had little effect except with higher concentrations of alcohol, possibly explicable on its higher melting point. Cheese was less effective than milk; but it was emphasized that the cheese used probably had a very low fat content, as it was obtained during the War. Since meat also was found to delay absorption, it can be concluded that both fat and protein are effective. This effect of protein, and amino acids as well, in reducing the maximal concentration of alcohol in the blood after a dose of alcohol was confirmed by Widmark (9, 10). He found that, in addition to lowering the maximum concentration, the period during which alcohol remained in the blood was reduced. In other words, the blood alcohol curve was lower throughout, and reached the base line sooner, than when no protein or amino acid accompanied the alcohol. From this he assumed that there was an actual removal of a portion of the alcohol from metabolism, probably by a combination of some sort with the amino acids, possibly esterification. Haggard and Greenberg (11) disagreed with this hypothesis, although the results they obtained were essentially similar to those of Widmark. They believe that the whole effect may be explained entirely on the basis of a slowing of absorption. The more rapid disappearance of alcohol from the blood, which appears to be a stumbling block to such an explanation, they surmount by saying that such is the slowing of absorption that with relatively small doses as used by Widmark the blood alcohol concentration falls prematurely to zero because the rate of combustion of the alcohol exceeds its rate of absorption, and consequently it does not accumulate in the blood or tissues. This ingenious explanation fails to explain, however, why the blood alcohol curve falls to zero equally rapidly when either the alcohol or the amino acid, or both, are administered intravenously and absorption can no longer play a part (12). Of this we shall say more when discussing the rate of metabolism of alcohol. Suffice it to say that protein has been demonstrated to slow absorption of alcohol but that the mechanism of this action is not well established.

Any effect of carbohydrates on alcohol absorption is due to their mechanical effect in slowing the emptying of the stomach. Administered as sugars in solution, when the mechanical effect is eliminated, we shall see that certain effects on the rate of alcohol metabolism are claimed but that absorption is not affected.

This effect of food in slowing absorption of alcohol, and thus reducing the maximum concentration attained after a given dose, is entirely in accord with the experience of those who have imbibed alcohol under varying conditions of relationship to meals. Whether the lesser effect of the same dose of alcohol taken with food is entirely to be ascribed to this delay in absorption or there is also to be invoked an effect on alcohol metabolism and perhaps on the resistance of nervous tissue to the effect of a given concentration of alcohol will receive consideration later.

Emotional state.—Another factor in the absorption of alcohol that has not been adequately investigated is the effect of the mood of the individual during the period of imbibition. It is more than probable that changes in sympathetic tone incidental to the emotional state may have a considerable effect on gastric motility, and thus on alcohol absorption.

Habituation.—It is rather surprising to note that one of the factors influencing the rate of absorption of alcohol is the amount of alcohol habitually consumed. Nor is the effect of habituation to alcohol one of slowing of absorption, as one might presume as a result of chronic gastric irritation, but rather of an increased rate of absorption. Thus Schmidt (13) followed the blood alcohol concentration after a dose of alcohol of 0.6 cc. per kilogram in a group of abstainers and a similar group of habituated individuals. There was a very considerable variation from individual to individual; but on the average the maximum concentration was higher, and was attained more rapidly, in the habituated group than in the abstainers. In accord with this is the work of Fleming and Stotz (14), who administered a dose of 0.6 cc. of alcohol as a 20% solution to 25 heavy drinkers, 15 moderate drinkers, and 12 abstainers. Following the blood alcohol concentration subsequent to ingestion, no difference was found between the curves of the moderate drinkers and the abstainers; but in the case of the heavy drinkers the blood alcohol concentration rose more rapidly and reached a higher maximum. Miles (6) also came to the conclusion that confirmed drinkers seemed to absorb alcohol more quickly, particularly when the concentration of alcohol ingested was high. Bernhard and Goldberg (15) gave doses of .44 to .79 gm. of alcohol per kilogram as a 36–45% solution to abstainers and alcoholics, and found that on the average the habituated individuals showed a more rapid rise of the blood alcohol curve with a higher maximum. They note, however, that there is sufficient overlap between the groups to make a diagnosis of chronic alcoholism on the basis of the curve of blood alcohol concentration impossible. Newman and Card (16) habituated three dogs by allowing them to consume 6.8 cc. of alcohol per kilogram daily in their drinking water over a period of thirteen months. At the end of the period of habituation they were given a test dose of 4.0 cc. per kilogram by stomach tube, and on another occasion the same dose intravenously, and the curves of blood alcohol so obtained were compared with those of a group of three abstinent dogs subjected to the same test procedures. As can be seen from Figure 1 the blood alcohol concentration rose more rapidly and to a higher maximum in the habituated dogs. In fact, if we disregard the sample taken at one hour, the curve in the habituated animals is almost identical with that after intravenous administration, indicating rapid and complete absorption. In the case of the control animals, however, the concentration attained after oral administration is definitely inferior to that after intravenous injection. Whether or not this indicates incomplete absorption of alcohol in these dogs it is impossible to say, as unfortunately the alcohol concentrations were not followed until they attained the base line. Searching for an explanation for the more rapid

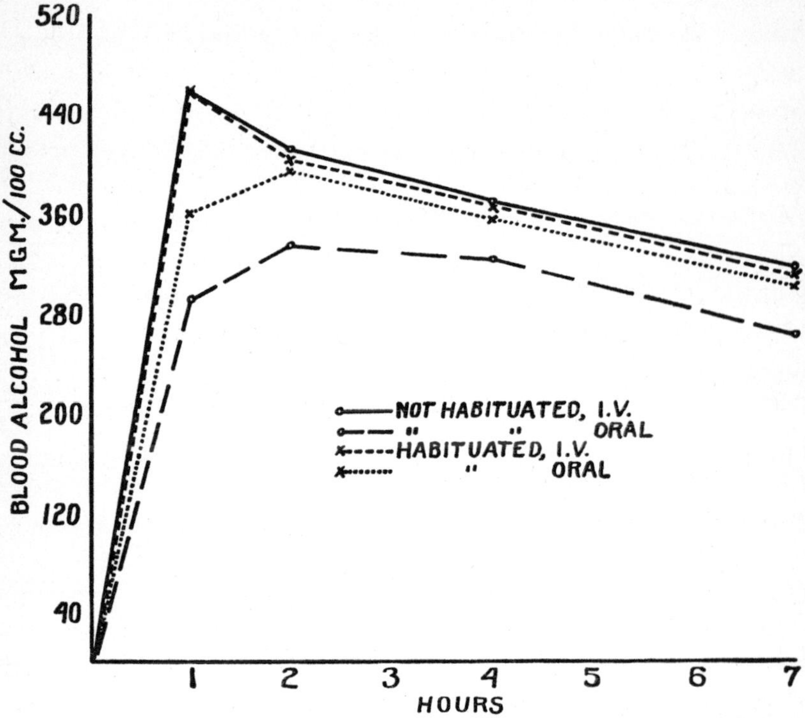

FIG. 1.—Blood alcohol concentration after oral and intravenous administration of 4 cc. per kilogram of alcohol to habituated and nonhabituated dogs (Newman and Card).

absorption in habituated subjects, the habituated dogs were given 300 cc. of a barium mixture by stomach tube and the time at which this had disappeared from the stomach was determined fluoroscopically. The emptying time of the stomach so determined was 75 minutes for the three habituated dogs, and 150 minutes for five normal controls. Thus it is evident that at least part of the increased rate of absorption of alcohol by habituated subjects is due to more rapid emptying of the stomach.

Rate of absorption.—The actual speed at which alcohol administered on an empty stomach is absorbed is not agreed upon by all workers. We have seen that the concentration and form in which the alcohol is administered affect its rate of absorption. It is generally held that around 90% of moderate doses of diluted alcohol administered within a short period is absorbed in the first hour, and that of this amount probably a considerable proportion is absorbed in the first twenty minutes. Other workers, however, controvert this, maintaining that absorption continues in significant degree for as much as six hours after administration. Thus Haggard and Greenberg (17), in an effort to reconcile their findings regarding the rate of metabolism of alcohol with those of Mellanby (7), a subject with which we shall deal at length in the next chapter, state: "Mellanby assumed that absorption is complete at the time the concentration of alcohol in the blood reaches its maximum. In fact, however, on the contrary our finding that the rate of oxidation is not absolute but relative requires us to recognize as a corollary that absorption is really a prolonged process. The slow absorption of alcohol, thus revealed, unfortunately cannot be determined by direct experiment. But it can be derived mathematically from our data." This they proceed to do. Their conclusion is that after the fifth or sixth hour absorption is complete.

Harger, Hulpieu, and Lamb (18) subsequently were able to accomplish what Haggard and Greenberg stated "unfortunately cannot be determined by direct experiment," that is, a demonstration of the rate of absorption of alcohol from the gastrointestinal tract. They determined the concentrations of alcohol in the alimentary tract and in the blood at intervals after the administration of varying doses of alcohol orally and intravenously. They found that in those animals killed two hours or more after oral administration of alcohol equilibrium had been reached between the alcohol concentration of the intestinal tract and the tissues. However, a certain amount of alcohol remained in the intestinal tract—5.12% of the total body alcohol in eight dogs—as would be expected when we recall that alcohol is absorbed by diffusion and that when there is no longer a diffusion gradient between the gut and the tissues further absorption will not take place. However, as the concentration in the tissues is decreased by combustion of alcohol, a new equilibrium will be established by diffusion of further alcohol from the intestine, and so on until alcohol finally disappears simultaneously from both intestinal contents and tissues. Thus the intestinal content acts as a storehouse for a part of the alcohol in the body, just as do tissues which do not participate in alcohol metabolism. This storage of alcohol was shown to take place when alcohol was administered intravenously equally with when it was given orally. Taking this into consideration, the authors determined the amount of unabsorbed alcohol as the amount in the alimentary tract in excess of that which would be present after intravenous administration. On this basis they found that with a dose of 0.5 gm. per kilogram 93.8% was absorbed in the first half-hour, compared with 57.3% with a dose of 3.0 gm. and 50.9% with 6.0 gm. With the 3.0 gm. dose 89.9% was absorbed at 1 hour, 93.2% at 1½ hours, 96.5% at 2 hours, and 99.0% at 3 hours. Thus we see that increasing the amount of alcohol to be absorbed results in a longer time being required for its absorption, but that with a relatively large dose such as 3.0 gm. per kilogram 90% is absorbed in 1 hour and complete absorption has taken place in 3 hours. This evidence, obtained directly in a carefully controlled study, must be admitted to overrule the mathematical deductions of Haggard and Greenberg, more especially since they are in accord with those of all other workers in the field. Thus Jungmichel (19) found the peak of blood alcohol concentration after administration of 0.5 cc. per kilogram to human subjects to occur from 40 to 60 minutes after ingestion, while Newman and Card (16) found the peak of blood alcohol concentration after oral administration of 4.0 cc. per kilogram in dogs to occur between 1 and 2 hours after ingestion.

Inhibition of absorption.—Hanzlik (5), working with isolated loops of intestine, found that absorption proceeded at the same rate in cats and dogs. The size of the loop seemed to exert little influence, an increase of six times in its length effecting an increase in absorption of but 10%. Using the same animal, he injected an equal amount of alcohol into a number of intestinal loops and excised them for alcohol analysis at intervals of from 10 minutes to 2 hours. At 10 minutes 53% of the alcohol had disappeared, at 30 minutes 78%, and at 1 and 2 hours 84%. Thus the initial rapid absorption of alcohol seemingly inhibited subsequent absorption. When a loop was injected and then excised just before injection of a second loop, no effect was apparent on absorption from the second loop. From this evidence it was concluded that the inhibition was a local phenomenon. Slow intravenous injection of 1 cc. per kilogram was effective in slowing absorption by 13%, while rapid intravenous injection was less effective and a control injection of saline entirely without effect. Changes in systemic blood pressure had no effect on absorption. Vasoconstriction with ice, epinephrine, or strophanthus slowed absorption, as did the decrease in permeability brought about by calcium chloride and formaldehyde. Irritants such as mustard and trauma increased absorption. An effort was made to measure circulation time in the intestine, and it was shown that alcohol injected intravenously was effective in slowing the circulation about 50%. However, alcohol injected into the intestinal loops failed to bring about any significant slowing of the circulation. No definite conclusions regarding the mechanism for this inhibition of absorption of alcohol could be made; but it was felt that two factors probably played a part: first, a slowing of the circulation in the gut; and, second, the "binding" of an initial high concentration of alcohol by the gut wall, reducing the diffusion gradient between the wall and the contents, and thus slowing absorption. The practical importance of this work, differing as it does from that of Harger, Hulpieu, and Lamb (18) in the intact animal, is questionable. However, it is of interest that Edkins and Murray (20) reported findings essentially similar to those of Hanzlik. They used decerebrate cats, and injected 8% alcohol in Ringer's solution into an isolated section of intestine 55 cm. in length located 8 inches below the pylorus. The amount of liquid absorbed in two twenty-minute periods was definitely less with alcohol and Ringer's solution than with Ringer's solution alone, and the inhibition of absorption was more marked in the second twenty-minute period than in the first. They conclude from this that alcoholic beverages should be less thirst-quenching than plain water.

Just what the mechanism of this inhibition of absorption may be is difficult to say. It seems to be much more apparent in isolated loops of intestine than when alcohol has access to the whole gastrointestinal tract. The presence of alcohol in the intestinal wall may, through some vasomotor mechanism, be effective in slowing the circulation to the gut. This would allow the local blood alcohol concentration to more nearly approximate that in the intestinal contents, with a lower diffusion gradient and consequently slower absorption. Also, alcohol may, as suggested by Hanzlik (5), be in some manner "fixed" in the mucosa so as not readily to diffuse into the blood stream. The resultant high alcohol concentration in the intestinal wall would lower the diffusion gradient between wall and contents and so retard further absorption of alcohol. Both of these explanations are as yet purely hypothetical, having no adequate experimental basis. One thing is definite, and that is that a certain amount of alcohol will remain in the intestinal contents so long as there is alcohol present in the blood stream, since without a gradient between the intestinal contents and the blood no diffusion will take place. Since the intestinal contents in some animals constitute a considerable proportion of the body weight, this amount of alcohol may be relatively large and would account for the presence of unabsorbed alcohol in the gut long after the initial active period of absorption has passed.

Sympathomimetic drugs.—The recent work of Rinkel and Myerson (29) on the effect of sympathomimetic substances on alcohol absorption, which might well be taken as a model for this type of investigation, has demonstrated the importance of vasomotor changes in this regard. Using 15 human subjects, patients in a mental hospital having had no access to alcohol, they gave doses of from .5 to .66 gm. of alcohol per kilogram by mouth, by duodenal tube, and intravenously. Simultaneous injection or ingestion of benzedrine, paredrine, epinephrine, and atropine all were effective in slowing the absorption of orally administered alcohol, as evidenced by the shape of the blood alcohol curve, the effectiveness of the various agents being in the order listed. That the effect was one on absorption rather than metabolism was shown by the lack of effect on the curve of blood alcohol after intravenous administration of alcohol. There was some slowing of absorption, but by no means as great as with oral administration, when the alcohol was given directly into the duodenum. From this the authors concluded that the slowing of alcohol absorption brought about by these agents is due in part to retardation of emptying of the stomach and in part to slowing of intestinal absorption, the most likely mechanism for the latter action being a slowing of blood flow to the gut. Unfortunately this is not capable of demonstration in the intact human subject; but animal experimentation and possibly also investigation in patients who have had a laparotomy may be expected to provide the necessary evidence.

Methods of investigation.—It has been apparent that there are several avenues of approach to the investigation of speed of alcohol absorption. Least physiologic of these is the isolated-intestinal-loop method. An equally direct appraisal may be made in laboratory animals by administering a known amount of alcohol and sacrificing the animal at some definite interval thereafter. Analysis of the carcass and of the intestinal contents separately reveals the amount of alcohol absorbed in a direct and accurate manner. Allowance must be made, as pointed out by Harger, Hulpieu, and Lamb (18), for the amount of alcohol remaining in the intestinal contents in equilibrium with the alcohol in the body tissues and which would be present there even if the alcohol were administered parenterally. This method is direct and incontrovertible, but is extravagant of animals, as the fact that one animal is utilized for only one concentration of alcohol and one time interval requires the use of many of them if a smooth curve of amount of alcohol absorbed against time is to be obtained. Another approach, applicable to man as well, depends on the fact, which we shall discuss at length later on, that after the active period of absorption the alcohol concentration of the blood decreases at a constant rate. Because of this it can be fairly safely assumed that when the curve of blood alcohol concentration against time assumes this constant rate of decline the greater part of absorption has already taken place. This type of work, although less direct than the others, has the great advantage of being much more expeditious; and furthermore it is applicable to human subjects. The agreement of results between the last two methods has been so good that the indirect method can be accepted as quite suitable for further investigation.

Concentration in blood from various sites.—Since, as we have seen, absorption of alcohol takes place largely from the small intestine, the absorbed alcohol is conveyed by the portal system directly to the liver. During the period of active absorption the alcohol concentration of the blood in the portal vein is higher than that in the body in general. Thus Falconer and Gladnikoff (21) found the alcohol concentration in the portal blood of rabbits receiving alcohol to be higher than that determined simultaneously in the caval blood. The blood in the hepatic vein contains less alcohol than that in the portal vein, partly because of diffusion of alcohol into the liver substance and to a lesser extent because of metabolism of some of the alcohol by the liver cells. This concentration is further reduced in the inferior vena cava by dilution with blood from the systemic circulation of the lower part of the body, and still further after junction with the superior vena cava before the right auricle is reached. During circulation through the lungs a certain amount of alcohol is lost by diffusion into the lung tissue, while some is excreted by diffusion into the alveolar air, which is subsequently expired. Thus the alcohol concentration in the left side of the heart is somewhat, but not greatly, lower than that in the right. The concentration in the arterial blood is reduced as it passes through the capillary network, so that during the period of active absorption venous blood may contain significantly less alcohol than arterial blood. This difference is greater the more rapidly absorption is taking place, and disappears when equilibrium is reached between the blood and tissues. The slowest of the tissues to reach equilibrium with the blood is muscle, as was shown in dogs by Harger, Hulpieu, and Lamb (18). Thus it follows that during the active period of absorption the alcohol concentration of the venous blood from the extremities, which incidentally is that usually secured for analysis, will be less than that in either arterial blood or venous blood from those organs in which equilibrium is established most rapidly, such as the brain. Thus during this period venous blood alcohol concentration from the extremities will reflect, not the alcohol concentration in the blood supplying the brain, but rather this concentration less the loss by diffusion into the not yet filled muscular reservoir. The extent of this difference is related to the rapidity with which absorption takes place, and would be greatest in the first half-hour after ingestion of a large dose of alcohol on an empty stomach. Under these circumstances, which rarely occur in social drinking, absorption would be fairly complete within an hour, and equilibrium with the muscles certainly within another hour; so that after this period venous blood from an extremity would yield approximately the same alcohol concentration as cerebral arterial blood. When alcohol is consumed in repeated small doses, usually accompanied by food, as is the usual custom, the difference between venous and arterial blood, even during the period of active absorption, is probably never significant, as equilibration can proceed apace with the slower absorption under these conditions. Thus for all practical purposes venous blood from an extremity secured an hour or more after imbibition can be assumed to reflect faithfully the alcohol content of the cerebral circulation. Haggard and Greenberg (22) have stressed the importance of this difference in alcohol concentration of blood from different sources. They found that during the first hour after ingestion of a large dose, 3 gm. per kilogram, by a dog, the venous blood from a leg was notably inferior in alcohol content to the arterial blood, with capillary blood intermediate between them. After intravenous injection, however, they found equilibrium to be attained within fifteen minutes after the injection was completed. This rapid equilibration after intravenous injection would hardly be compatible with the muscle-lag hypothesis of Harger, Hulpieu, and Lamb, which Haggard and Greenberg anticipated without any experimental proof, did one not take into consideration the extremely slow rate of injection used. Thus they required one and a half hours to administer 3 gm. per kilogram, so that entry into the blood was notably slower than with oral administration. Haggard and Greenberg claimed that more rapid injection resulted in death of the dogs. Just why the dogs should die when their blood alcohol concentration is raised at the same rate and to the same height by intravenous injection as one would feel perfectly safe in achieving by oral administration is hard to say. Nor, in fact, in a considerable experience of administering this same dosage to dogs by the intravenous route have we had any mortality using a rate of injection approximately three times this rapid. Thus we will have to leave this along with certain other findings of these authors among our unsolved mysteries.

Lag of equilibration in muscle.—Whether the lag in equilibration in muscle mentioned by Haggard and Greenberg and shown experimentally by Harger, Hulpieu, and Lamb has even the significance we have accorded it is open to question from the theoretical viewpoint. It must be recalled that the latter authors specified that after administration of alcohol the animals were restrained until they were killed, while it is doubtful if the animals of Haggard and Greenberg had much opportunity for exercise when three to five specimens of blood from different sites were being taken every half-hour. Since the blood flow through muscle varies tremendously with activity, it is quite possible that under more normal conditions the muscle lag, which may be attributed to the small amount of circulation through resting muscles, would no longer be apparent. This problem is readily amenable to investigation; for example, a crucial experiment would consist of giving an anesthetized dog a dose of say 3 gm. per kilogram by stomach tube, following which one leg would be "exercised" by repeated faradic stimulation while the other would be left alone. At the end of fifteen or thirty minutes samples of muscle from each side would be analyzed for alcohol, and arterial blood by cardiac puncture obtained. If speed of circulation is the important factor, we would expect the alcohol content of the exercised leg to exceed that of the quiescent one and more nearly to approach that of the arterial blood. Also, the effect of exercise on the curve of blood alcohol after a dose of alcohol on an empty stomach in man warrants investigation, not from the standpoint of exercise increasing the rate of alcohol metabolism, which it has been shown repeatedly not to do, but from that of lowering the peak of concentration incidental to equilibration failing to keep pace with absorption.

Rate of equilibration.—Le Breton (23) found that after intravenous injection of 0.5 to 2.5 gm. per kilogram in the cat or rabbit 20 to 60 minutes were required for equilibration. Her definition of equilibration is, however, somewhat different from that of other workers, it being defined as the point at which no more alcohol is leaving the blood than is being burned in the tissues. Naturally this point cannot be reached until active absorption has ceased, and consequently if absorption is very slow the time recorded may be much more dependent on absorption of alcohol into the blood than on equilibration of alcohol between blood and tissues. It was found that with fasting dogs equilibrium was attained an hour after ingestion of a dose of alcohol, while if a meal had been consumed four hours previously 130 minutes were required. In rabbits, either fasting or otherwise, more than five hours were required for equilibration, while in the fasting rat equilibrium was attained in one hour. With a meal of carbohydrate this was lengthened to 90 minutes, and with meat to 100 minutes. It can be seen that rabbits are for this reason, if no other, poor animals for alcohol experimentation.

The relative rapidity with which equilibrium is attained in the tissues in man is well demonstrated by Figure 2, which shows

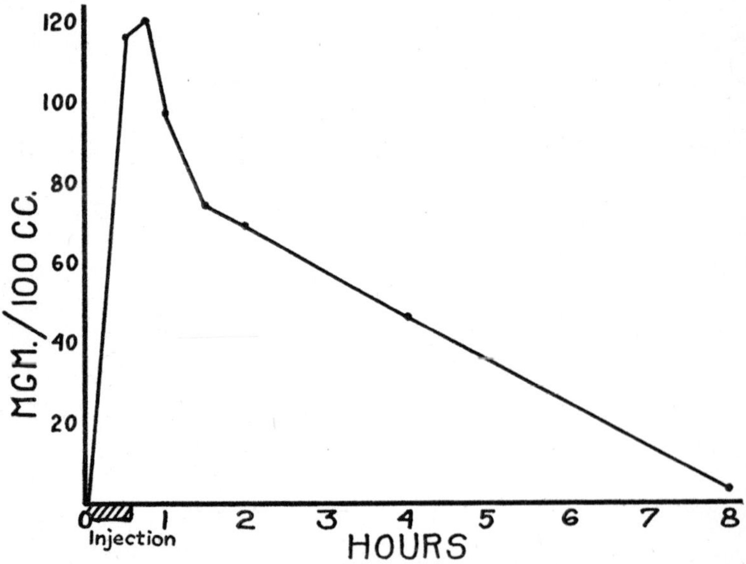

FIG. 2.—Blood alcohol concentration after intravenous injection of 1 cc. per kilogram of alcohol in man (Mehrtens and Newman).

the curve of blood alcohol concentration against time after intravenous injection. A peak occurs during the injection, its height being determined by the speed of injection; but this levels off within approximately an hour to assume the straight-line decline characteristic of the disappearance of alcohol from the blood when this is due in large measure to its combustion.

Concentration in various tissues.—The concentration of alcohol attained in the various tissues after equilibrium has been established is not equal throughout the body. Harger, Hulpieu, and Lamb (18) determined the alcohol content of various tissues when equilibration had taken place after orally administered alcohol. They found that under these conditions the alcohol concentration of the tissues was essentially the same as after intravenous administration, indicating that tissue distribution of alcohol is not in any way dependent on the route of administration. It was shown that although the absolute concentration of alcohol in brain, liver, muscle, stomach tissue, upper intestine, and lower intestine showed some variation, the amount of alcohol per gram of water in all of these tissues was essentially the same. Blood and stomach contents they found to store somewhat more alcohol than the other tissues on this basis. Miles (6) found that plasma contained as much as 50% more alcohol than whole blood, obtaining his samples from man after ingestion of small doses of alcohol. Newman and Abramson (24) found a greater concentration of alcohol in plasma than in red cells; but the difference was in the order of approximately 30%, giving a difference between plasma and whole blood of but 15% in contrast to the 50% found by Miles. This difference they found to be the same whether the blood was obtained from alcoholized men or the alcohol was added to human blood in vitro. Also they showed that if blood containing alcohol was centrifuged, and the red cells resuspended in plasma containing no alcohol, determination of the alcohol content of this plasma showed a higher concentration than remained in the red cells, and that this equilibrium was reached in but a few minutes. Thus the partition of alcohol between cells and plasma seems to be on a basis of solubility rather than on any vital function. That total water content alone does not determine the amount of alcohol in the various tissues has been demonstrated by Nicloux, who has evolved a theory that some of the water in tissues is "bound," and cannot participate in the competition for alcohol.

The ratio of alcohol concentrations of blood and brain was shown by Harger, Hulpieu, and Lamb (18) to be 1.18 on an average in 12 dogs. The range was from 1.32 to .97. Newman and Lehman (25) found a somewhat higher figure, 1.35, for rats. The relationship between the concentrations in blood and spinal fluid is somewhat more complex, for the reason that the spinal fluid represents a rather inert reservoir, with relatively small surface for interchange. Thus Mehrtens and Newman (26) showed that after intravenous injection of a dose of alcohol in man the concentration of alcohol in the lumbar spinal fluid lagged behind that in the blood during the period of increment of blood alcohol, while during the period of decrement the spinal-fluid concentration equaled and then surpassed that of the blood. When fluid was obtained from the cisterna magna instead of the lumbar region, this lag was much less apparent, as seen in Figure 3, which the authors interpreted as evidence that the

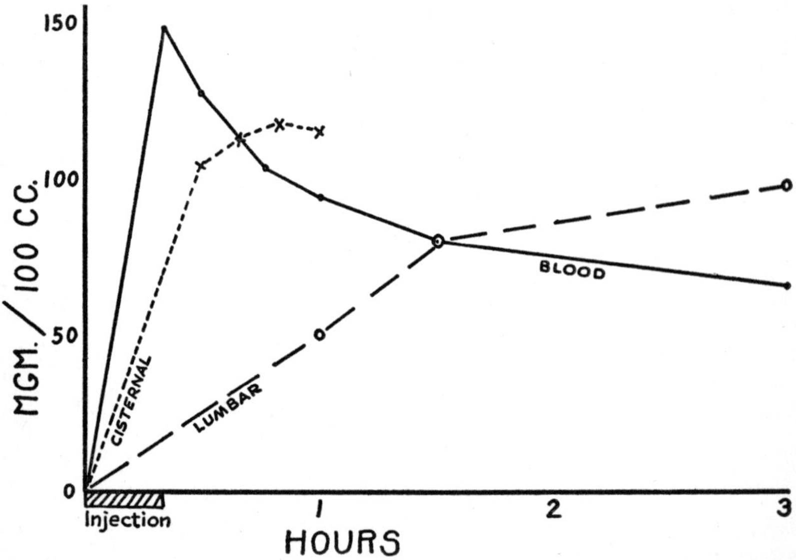

FIG. 3.—Blood, cisternal, and lumbar-fluid alcohol concentration after intravenous injection of 1 cc. per kilogram of alcohol in man (Mehrtens and Newman).

major portion of the alcohol gained access to the spinal fluid at the cephalic end of the system, the spinal subarachnoid space acting as an inert reservoir. When the change in concentration of blood alcohol was eliminated by a slow intravenous drip to maintain the blood alcohol constant over a period of five hours after the initial injection, simultaneous determinations of the alcohol concentrations of the blood plasma, lumbar fluid, and cisternal fluid at the end of that period showed that in the majority of instances the cisternal and lumbar-fluid concentrations were approximately equal and surpassed the concentration in the plasma by an appreciable amount. This brought up the possibility of an active secretion of alcohol into the spinal fluid. Whether this need be postulated or the difference in solubility of alcohol in the spinal fluid and plasma is sufficient to account for the difference found in vivo should be subjected to experimental determination in vitro.

Relation of dose to blood alcohol concentration.—From this unequal distribution of alcohol throughout the tissues it is obvious that the blood alcohol concentration after a given dose of alcohol is not equal to that which would ensue were the alcohol merely dissolved in a mass of water equal to the body weight, but rather is dependent on the relative masses of the different tissues and the solubility of alcohol in each. Haggard and Greenberg (17) call attention to this fact, which had, however, been worked out in considerable detail by Widmark (27) some time previously.

Widmark followed the blood alcohol concentration in the post-absorptive phase in man and in dogs, and confirmed the observation of Mellanby (7) that the rate of decline was constant in relation to time. He felt, therefore, that the theoretical concentration of alcohol in the blood immediately after ingestion, assuming that absorption were immediate and complete, might be obtained by extrapolation of this linear post-absorptive curve by simple extension at the same slope to the axis of ordinates, as seen in Figure 4. This purely hypothetical figure he designated c_o. Now if absorbed alcohol were distributed uniformly throughout the body, c_o expressed in milligrams per gram of blood should be equal to the dose A in grams of alcohol di-

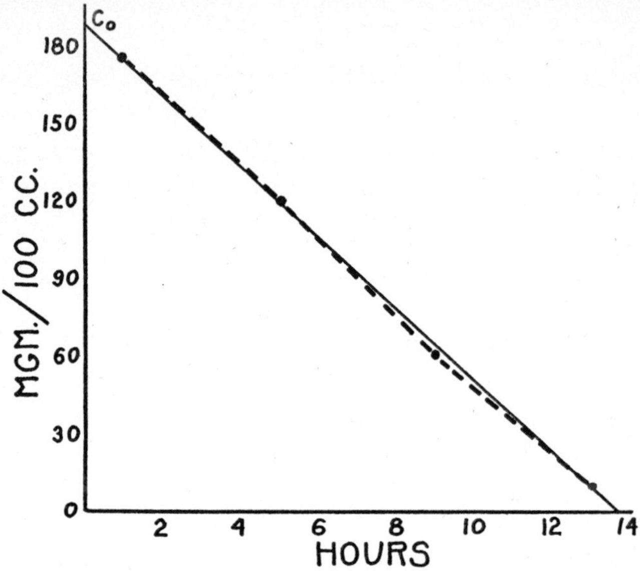

FIG. 4.—Blood alcohol concentration after intravenous injection of 1.5 gm. per kilogram of alcohol in a dog, illustrating extrapolation of the curve to the hypothetical concentration c_o at zero time (Newman and Lehman).

vided by the body weight p in kilograms, or $c_o = \frac{A}{p}$. Widmark found that, as we should expect, this was not true, and that it was necessary to multiply body weight p by a factor r for the relationship to hold, so that the equation became $c_o = \frac{A}{p \cdot r}$. This factor r was dependent on the relative proportions of the various tissues in the animal body. It was found to be relatively constant for any one species, the value being determined by administering a dose of alcohol, determining blood alcohol concentration at intervals and, from the curve so obtained, the theoretical value c_o by extrapolation. From this value and the known data r

was determined from the formula $r = \dfrac{A}{p \cdot c_o}$. r as determined in dogs averaged .75, in man .68. Newman and Lehman (28) similarly determined r for a number of species. They found the values for man to be .70, for dogs .79, for cats .74, for pigeons .68, and for chickens .89. It will be seen that the figures for men and dogs agree very well with those obtained by Widmark. This is especially noteworthy when it is taken into consideration that the route of administration was different, Widmark using the oral route and Newman and Lehman the intravenous. In rabbits, which had been known to be unusual in their metabolism of alcohol, Newman and Lehman found the factor r to exceed unity, especially with smaller doses of alcohol. Thus with a dose of 3 gm. per kilogram r averaged .97, while with half this dose it averaged 1.23. The finding of an r exceeding unity can have but two meanings: either alcohol is stored in some tissue at a concentration higher than that which exists in the blood, or a certain amount of alcohol is very rapidly destroyed after administration. That this rapid rate of destruction of alcohol does not continue for any length of time was shown by the rate of fall of the blood alcohol curve, which followed the orthodox straight-line form. The storage of alcohol in a concentration higher than that in the blood is contrary to the experimental findings in other animals. Thus we have no valid explanation for this aberrant finding in rabbits, which certainly merits further investigation. Until it is satisfactorily explained, however, rabbits must be considered unsuitable for alcohol experimentation, at least if findings are to be applied to other species.

Thus we see that the distribution of alcohol in the animal body is for a given species sufficiently constant to permit a fairly accurate prediction of the blood alcohol concentration after any given dosage of alcohol. Since, as we shall see later, the rate of fall of this concentration is also fairly constant, the blood alcohol concentration at any time after ingestion may be predicted with considerable accuracy.

REFERENCES

1. Faiteberg, R., and Medevedew, B., "The Rate of Absorption of Alcohol from the Pawlow Pouch," *Ukrainian Biochem. J.*, **8**:190, 1935, *Physiol. Abstr.*, **21**:583, 1936
2. Edkins, N., and Murray, N. M., "Influence of Carbon Dioxide on the Absorption of Alcohol by the Gastric Mucosa," *J. Physiol.*, **59**:271, 1924
3. Higgins, H. L., "The Rapidity with Which Alcohol and Some Sugars May Serve as Nutriment," *Am. J. Physiol.*, **41**:258, 1916
4. Cori, C. F., Villiaume, E. L., and Cori, G. T., "The Absorption of Ethyl Alcohol," *J. Biol. Chem.*, **87**:19, 1930
5. Hanzlik, P. J., and Collins, R. J., "The Absorption of Alcohol," *J. Pharmacol.*, **5**:185, 1913
6. Miles, W. R., "The Comparative Concentrations of Alcohol in Human Blood and Urine at Intervals after Ingestion," *J. Pharmacol.*, **20**:265, 1922
7. Mellanby, E., *Alcohol: Its Absorption into and Disappearance from the Blood under Different Conditions*, National Research Council (Great Britain) Special Report Series, No. 31, 1919
8. Newman, H. W., and Van Winkle, W., Jr., unpublished data
9. Widmark, E. M. P., "Der Einfluss des Nahrungbestandteile auf den Alkoholgehalt des Blutes," *Biochem. Zeit.*, **267**:128, 1933
10. Widmark, E. M. P., "Über die Einwirkung von Aminosauren aud des Alkoholgehalt des Blutes," *Biochem. Zeit.*, **265**:237, 1933
11. Haggard, H. W., and Greenberg, L. A., "Studies on Absorption, Distribution, and Elimination of Alcohol, Influence of Glycocol upon Absorption of Alcohol," *J. Pharmacol.*, **68**:482, 1940
12. Newman, H. W., unpublished data
13. Schmidt, M., "Alcohol Studies: II. Concentration of Alcohol in the Blood," *J. Ind. Hyg.*, **16**:355, 1934
14. Fleming, R., and Stotz, E., "The Blood and Spinal Fluid Alcohol in Abstainers, Chronic Alcoholics, and in the Psychoses, *J. Nerv. and Ment. Dis.*, **80**:327, 1934
15. Bernhard, C. G., and Goldberg, L., "Aufnahme und Verbrennung des Alkohols bei Alkoholisten," *Acta Med. Scand.*, **86**:152, 1935
16. Newman, H. W., and Card, J. F., "The Nature of Tolerance to Ethyl Alcohol," *J. Nerv. and Ment. Dis.*, **86**:428, 1937
17. Haggard, H. W., and Greenberg, L. A., "Studies in Absorption, Distribution, and Elimination of Ethyl Alcohol, Rate of Oxidation of Alcohol in the Body," *J. Pharmacol.*, **52**:174, 1934
18. Harger, R. N., Hulpieu, H. R., and Lamb, E. B., "The Speed with Which Various Parts of the Body Reach Equilibrium in the Storage of Ethyl Alcohol," *J. Biol. Chem.*, **120**:689, 1937
19. Jungmichel, G., "Die Resorption von Athylalkohol unter besonderer Beruchsichtigung bei Alkoholgewohnung," *Arch. Exptl. Path. Pharmakol.*, **173**:388, 1933
20. Edkins, N., and Murray, N. M., "The Effect of Carbon Dioxide on the Absorption of Alcohol and the Influence of Alcohol on the Diffusion of Carbon Dioxide in the Small Intestine," *J. Physiol.*, **62**:13, 1926

21. FALCONER, B., and GLADNIKOFF, H., "Alcohol Values in Blood from Different Localities in Rabbits," *Skand. Arch. Physiol.*, **68**:245, 1934
22. HAGGARD, H. W., and GREENBERG, L. A., "Studies in the Absorption, Distribution, and Elimination of Ethyl Alcohol, the Excretion of Alcohol in Urine and Expired Air; and the Distribution of Alcohol between Air and Water, Blood and Urine," *J. Pharmacol.*, **52**:150, 1934
23. LE BRETON, E., "Vitesse de diffusion de l'alcool ethylique dans l'organisme selon la voie d'introduction; dose administrée et concentration realisée au niveau de tissues," *Compt. rend. soc. biol.*, **117**:704, 1934
24. NEWMAN, H. W., and ABRAMSON, M., unpublished data
25. NEWMAN, H. W., and LEHMAN, A. J., "Nature of Acquired Tolerance to Alcohol," *J. Pharmacol.*, **62**:301, 1938
26. MEHRTENS, H. G., and NEWMAN, H. W., "Alcohol Injected Intravenously; Its Penetration into the Cerebrospinal Fluid in Man," *Arch. Neurol. Psychiatry*, **30**:1092, 1933
27. WIDMARK, E. M. P., "Verteilung und Umwandlung des Athylalkohols im Organismus des Hundes," *Biochem. Zeit.*, **267**:128, 1933
28. NEWMAN, H. W., and LEHMAN, A. J., "Rate of Disappearance of Alcohol from the Blood Stream in Various Species," *Arch. intern. pharmacodynamie*, **55**:440, 1937
29. RINKEL, M., and MYERSON, A., "Pharmacological Studies in Experimental Alcoholism. I. The Effect of Sympathomimetic Substances on the Blood-Alcohol Level in Man," *J. Pharmacol.*, **71**:75, 1941

CHAPTER II

EXCRETION

It may be said in general that the excretion of ethyl alcohol follows very simple laws. This is due to the fact that because of its ready diffusibility alcohol is found in almost all of the tissues and fluids of the body in approximately equal concentrations. Thus we might expect alcohol to be eliminated in the excreta in an amount dependent on the volume of the excrement and the concentration of alcohol in the body at the time of elimination; and this is essentially what occurs. Concentration of alcohol in the excreta probably does not occur, certainly not in any significant degree; and consequently it is not possible to increase the rate of excretion of alcohol except by increasing the volume of excreta, a measure which is subject to rather rigid restrictions.

Urinary excretion.—It was early shown that alcohol was eliminated to some degree in the urine. It has been extensively demonstrated that the concentration of alcohol in the urine bears a fixed relationship to the concentration in the blood, and that this concentration is entirely independent of the volume of urine excreted. There has been some controversy as to whether excretion by the kidney is by a process of simple diffusion or entails some degree of concentration by the kidney after filtration through the glomeruli. The basis for this controversy rests on the fact that the alcohol content of the urine in the post-absorptive period is invariably higher than that of venous blood obtained simultaneously. Thus Miles (1) gave human subjects a dose of 0.5 cc. per kilogram and found that, while for the first 20 to 30 minutes the concentration of alcohol in the urine was equal to that in the blood, subsequently it rose 30 to 50% above the blood concentration. He drew attention to the fact that plasma contains more alcohol than whole blood, but felt that even this difference was not sufficient to account for the higher urine values. It must be borne in mind that he was working with a dose of alcohol which gave quite low concentrations in the body fluids, a situation in which the accuracy of all methods of alcohol analysis is impaired and particularly where traces of other volatile oxidizable substances could lead to proportionately large errors.

Concentration in blood and urine.—The ratio of alcohol concentrations between blood and urine has been found by a number of investigators working independently to be approximately 1: 1.35, regardless of the actual concentration or of the species of the subject. Thus Jetter (2) analyzed the blood and urine of 372 patients admitted to hospital with a tentative diagnosis of acute alcoholism, and found the urine concentration to be usually higher, the average ratio being stated in the body of the paper to be 1: 1.23 and in the conclusions 1: 1.32, undoubtedly owing to an error in proofreading. Presumably the blood samples were obtained from an antecubital vein. No mention was made of how the urine samples were secured or over what period. The presumption is that with patients showing as high blood alcohol concentrations as did many of these, any sample the subject could produce, regardless of the time it had remained in the bladder, was acceptable. In this regard, Southgate and Carter (3) stress the difficulty in securing urine specimens from inebriates. They had to resort to the subterfuge of boarding up the regular lavatory in the cell (they were working in a police lockup), leaving the prisoner no choice but to use a urinal which delivered into a specimen bottle in the next room. Naturally, the specimens they got were hardly fresh bladder urine but rather represented what the prisoner had been holding until an opportunity presented itself for relinquishing it. It is thus reasonable to assume that such specimens probably reflected the blood alcohol concentration of some previous period, which was probably higher than that at the time of voiding. This presumption is based on a lack of ready diffusion of alcohol from the urine in the bladder into the blood, incidental to the small and poor absorbing surface presented in contrast to the large amount of fluid present. This presumption is supported by the recent work of Haggard *et al.* (10), who found that subjects who ingested whisky and held their urine over night showed no alcohol in the blood the next morning but still had a fairly high concentration of alcohol in the urine. Similarly, alcohol in a concentration of 0.2 to 0.4% instilled into the bladder showed a loss by absorption of but 5 to 7% in a two-hour period, while the agreement of curves of blood and urine alcohol obtained after ingestion by human subjects of 250 cc. of whisky depended largely on the frequency with which specimens were obtained, being good with short periods and poor with long. Southgate and Carter (3) gave 96 cc. of alcohol as an 8% solution to three human subjects, and secured blood and urine samples at the end of an hour. They found the average ratio of blood to urine to be 1: 1.32, and noted that the degree of diuresis had no effect on this ratio.

Mechanism of excretion by kidney.—The foregoing work seems to indicate a concentration of alcohol by the kidney. It is, however, quite possible to accept this ratio of blood to urine alcohol and still hold to the theory of simple diffusion, by the following line of reasoning: We have already seen that the blood plasma contains more alcohol than does whole blood, approximately in proportion to the greater amount of water in it. Since it is the plasma and not the formed elements of the blood which provides the fluid for the glomerular filtrate, we should expect this filtrate to reflect the concentration of the plasma rather than that of the whole blood. In addition, in collecting urine it is not possible to obtain that which is formed at precisely the time at which the blood specimen was taken. Certainly in man, unless one were to collect the urine specimens by ureteral catheterization, the voided urine must have been produced some time before the blood specimen was obtained. Since there is a steady rate of decline of blood alcohol concentration with time, we should expect this urine to reflect, not the concentration of alcohol in the plasma at the time it was collected, but rather the higher concentration that prevailed when it was excreted. Thus Smith and Stewart (4) reported that in animals, when urine samples were collected over a very short period, the ratio between blood and urine alcohol was unity, as contrasted with the situation in man when such collection is not feasible. The combination of these two factors is probably sufficient to account for the difference which has been consistently found between blood and urine alcohol concentrations, assuming that excretion is simply by diffusion, and that no concentration by the kidneys takes place. Haggard and Greenberg (5) are in accord with this theory. They found experimentally that alcohol is more soluble in urine than in blood in a ratio of 1.144 to 1. They gave a dose of 3 gm. alcohol per kilogram to two female dogs depressed with morphine, which had had ureteral catheters placed before being given the alcohol by stomach tube. Blood and urine samples were collected at intervals of from 20 to 160 minutes after ingestion, and analyzed for alcohol. The average ratio was almost precisely that of the differential solubility of the two fluids as observed in vitro. From this the authors concluded that excretion was by simple diffusion. Whether or not we care to accept this conclusion, which seems best supported by the facts, it remains that for all practical purposes it can be considered that alcohol exists in the urine in approximately the same concentration as in the blood plasma.

Amount of urinary excretion.—Since there is this constant relationship between the concentration of alcohol in the blood and urine, it follows that the amount of alcohol excreted is dependent in part on the concentration of alcohol in the blood, which in turn is roughly proportional to the amount of alcohol ingested. This dependence on the dose of alcohol is twofold, moreover, since not only the height to which the blood alcohol will rise but also the length of time that alcohol will remain in the body are dependent on the amount ingested. The latter factor is of importance in determining the amount of urine that will be excreted, which is roughly proportional to time, other factors remaining constant. Thus we can say that the amount of alcohol that will be excreted after a dose of alcohol is proportional to the average height of blood alcohol concentration during the time of sojourn of alcohol in the body, which is a function of the dose, and to the amount of urine excreted, which is a function of the time, which in turn is a function of the dose.

Other factors than the dose of alcohol may have a pronounced influence on the amount of alcohol excreted by the kidneys. Since the amount of urine excreted over any extended period is proportional to the fluid intake, other factors remaining constant, it will be seen that more alcohol will be excreted after the ingestion of dilute alcoholic beverages, such as beer, than when alcohol is taken in a more concentrated form, such as straight whisky. In addition to the fluid ingested with it, alcohol has been shown to be capable of producing a considerable diuresis. Maresca (6) reported a diuretic action of alcohol in abstainers and chronic alcoholics alike. MacNider and Donnelly (7) controlled the fluid intake of three dogs by administering 300 cc. of water twice a day by stomach tube for three days. On the fourth day they were given a dose of alcohol diluted to 300 cc. with water, and their urine output compared with that of the control days. The maximum increase in a three-hour period after ingestion was 211 cc., the minimum 84 cc. In this experiment the diuresis cannot be explained on a basis of increased water intake, since this was strictly controlled. Murray (8) administered 300 cc. of 10% alcohol to fasting human subjects at the same time of day in all cases, and found a definite and rapid diuretic action. Pituitrin, which inhibits water diuresis, presumably by decreasing capillary permeability, failed to overcome the diuretic effect of alcohol. In cats anesthetized with amytal, neither water nor alcohol produced a diuresis. Pituitrin was capable of bringing about a diuresis in these animals; but this was diminished when alcohol was given simultaneously. Although the author admits the results are difficult of explanation, she thinks that the evidence points to the diuresis from alcohol being an "exaggerated water diuresis." Thus the mechanism of the diuretic action of alcohol is far from clear. The development of transient albuminuria in the majority of MacNider and Donnelly's (7) dogs may be an indication that renal irritation plays some part. That the diuresis is not accompanied by any significant change in blood volume was shown by Levin (9), who administered 40 cc. of cognac by mouth or 25 cc. 33% alcohol in saline intravenously, and found by the trypan-red method that there was no change in blood volume in 3 cases, an increase averaging 38% in 3, and a decrease averaging 27% in 4.

It is probable that the diuretic effect of alcohol is responsible for the thirst universally experienced after an evening's drinking, and accounts for the reputation of alcohol as a "dehydrating agent," which it must be admitted it is, but not in the ordinary sense of the word. This diuretic action of alcohol, coupled with the fact that the ingestion of alcohol usually entails some increase in fluid intake over what would normally be the case, increases the urine output, and thus the excretion of alcohol through the kidneys.

The amount of alcohol that escapes the body through the renal channel has been determined experimentally by a number of investigators, with rather widely divergent results as would be expected from the variety of factors involved, but all falling within the range of from 1 to 5% of the amount ingested. Miles (1) recovered 1.2 to 1.6% from the urine in the first two hours after ingestion by human subjects of 0.5 cc. alcohol per kilogram, while Haggard and Greenberg (5) found as much as 4.3% after a dose of 4 gm. per kilogram in dogs.

Since we know that the concentration of alcohol in the urine is roughly proportional to that in the blood, and we can approximate the length of time alcohol will remain in the blood after any given dose of alcohol and thus what its average concentration over this period will be, and since we can estimate the amount of urine which will be excreted in this period, it should be possible from the data so calculated to ascertain crudely the amount of alcohol which on theoretical grounds we should expect to be excreted by the kidney. For example, let us assume that a 70-kilogram man ingests a pint of 100-proof whisky within a short period, say an hour. From Widmark's formula $c_o = \frac{A}{p \cdot r}$ we calculate that the theoretical initial concentration c_o, on the supposition that absorption were immediate and complete, would be 392 mgm.%. Now it has been satisfactorily demonstrated that the average rate of decline of this blood alcohol concentration is constant over the whole period during which alcohol is demonstrable in the blood stream, and that in man this is equal to .0023 mgm. per gram of blood per minute. Thus it would take approximately 24 hours (23 hours and 20 minutes, to be accurate) for all the alcohol to disappear. Since the disappearance is at a constant rate, we can say that the average blood alcohol concentration over this period is one-half of the theoretical maximum, or 196 mgm.%. The average amount of urine excreted by a man of this weight under ordinary circumstances is around 1,500 cc. Let us assume that with the increased ingestion of fluid and the diuretic action of the alcohol this is increased threefold, giving him an output of 4,500 cc. The total amount of alcohol eliminated in the urine should therefore be 45 $\times$ 196 mgm., or 8.82 gm. This is 4.6% of the amount ingested, and agrees quite well with the figure reported by Haggard and Greenberg (5) in dogs after a slightly higher dose.

A fact, however, which has been very generally overlooked is that the percentage of alcohol eliminated in the urine is not constant, but is dependent on the dosage, as we have already indicated. The reason for this is simple: not only the average blood alcohol level but also the period of sojourn of alcohol in the blood is proportional to the dose administered. Thus the *amount* of alcohol eliminated in the urine will be proportional to the square of the dose, and the *percentage* of the dose so eliminated will be proportional to the dose itself. This probably accounts for the rather wide divergence of results for urinary excretion of alcohol found by various workers. It must be kept in mind that this same condition holds equally for the elimination of alcohol by other excretory channels, and that the higher the dose of alcohol the higher will be the percentage excreted.

Elimination by the lungs.—Second, or perhaps equal, in importance to the urine in the elimination of alcohol is the breath. It has long been known that the distribution of volatile substances between the blood and the alveolar air follows Henry's law, and this is true for alcohol. Harger, Lamb, and Hulpieu (11) found that the alcohol content of 2 liters of expired air was equal on the average to that of 1 cc. of blood. The expired air does not contain the theoretical amount of alcohol in accord with Henry's law because it is not composed only of alveolar air, a certain variable percentage arising from the dead space incidental to the bronchial tree and upper air passages. Thus the amount, or percentage, of alveolar air in the expired air is dependent on the depth of respiration. In normal individuals this is sufficiently constant so that average experimentally determined figures are valid. When, however, there is alteration of respiratory rate and depth from any cause, such average values do not apply. The importance of this in connection with the use of breath in chemical determination of drunkenness we shall consider in a later chapter. Haggard and Greenberg (5) determined the alcohol concentration in blood, alveolar air, and expired air. They found that in the case of expired air the concentration was essentially that reported by Southgate and Carter (3), that is, 2 liters of expired air contained approximately the same amount of alcohol as 1 cc. of blood; but that the concentration of the alveolar air was, as would be expected, considerably higher, the ratio in that case being on the average 1,142: 1. It is of interest to note in this regard that the respiratory minute volume of their subjects varied between the rather close limits of from 3.8 to 4.8 liters, which probably accounts for the relative constancy of the relationship between expired air and blood demonstrated.

Amount excreted by lungs.—In general, it may be stated that 2 liters of expired air contains the same amount of alcohol as 1 cc. of blood. Thus we can compute, in the same manner as we did for urine, the theoretical amount of alcohol that would be eliminated in the breath after a given dose of alcohol. Let us assume the same conditions as before, that is, a 70-kilogram man and a pint of whisky—not an entirely unusual situation, and probably near the upper limit of ordinary human consumption. Let us further assume that he is at rest, or at least sedentary, which in view of the size of the dose is not an unwarranted assumption. Under these circumstances his minute volume of respiration will not exceed 7 liters. With an average blood alcohol concentration of 196 mgm.% over a period of approximately twenty-four hours we should expect him to pass a volume of 10,080 liters of air, with an average alcohol content of .98 mgm. per liter, or a total of 9.88 gm. of alcohol, which is 5.1% of the amount ingested. In consideration of the theoretical amount of alcohol to be eliminated by both the renal and pulmonary channels we have endeavored to err on the side of greater than probable values; yet if we add the amount eliminated by the two channels we find it to amount to but 9.7% of the dose ingested, which was a large one. Haggard and Greenberg (5) estimated a maximum of 7% could be eliminated through the breath, a figure based on their finding of an exponential rate of fall of blood alcohol concentration which we are inclined to doubt. The possibility of eliminating a significant amount of alcohol from the body by this channel in acute alcoholic intoxication will receive consideration in a later chapter.

Sweat.—Nyman and Palmlov (12) demonstrated that sweat contains approximately the same concentration of alcohol as does blood plasma. Since under normal conditions they estimated the amount of sweat eliminated in a day to be from 600 to 700 cc., it is obvious that less than 1% of ingested alcohol even after a large dose could be eliminated by this channel. Only under extreme conditions, such as in the tropics or a boiler room, would the secretion of sweat assume such proportions as to be a significant factor in the elimination of alcohol.

Saliva.—Alcohol also appears in the saliva, the concentration there approximating that of the blood. Thus Abels (13) found that when no alcohol was taken there was no volatile reducing substance in the saliva which would be determined as alcohol by the usual tests, while blood showed a "normal" alcohol content of from 0 to 7 mgm.%. In 50 inebriates, there was a deviation of plus or minus 10% between the alcohol concentrations of the blood and saliva. Friedemann, Motel, and Necheles (14) stress the importance of thoroughly rinsing the mouth before collection of the saliva samples, to eliminate chance contamination. Holding 20% alcohol in the mouth for one minute, following which it was expectorated, gave values up to 140 mgm.% in samples of saliva collected ten minutes later. By stomach tube, 100 cc. of 7% alcohol was given to 4 dogs, the animals being anesthetized with pentobarbital and prepared so that samples of saliva from the submaxillary duct, venous blood from the jugular vein, arterial blood from the carotid artery, and urine from a ureter were obtainable. It was found that the concentration in the saliva was midway between that in the venous and arterial blood, while that in the urine was higher than either. Three human subjects, fasting for 18 hours, were given 300 cc. of 7% alcohol by mouth, and samples of venous blood, saliva, and voided urine were obtained at intervals. The urine samples showed a concentration 32% higher than the blood, in accord with work we have already reported. Saliva alcohol concentration was 11% higher than venous blood alcohol, which is essentially what one would expect on the basis of their difference in water content. The maximum alcohol concentration was attained sooner in the saliva than in the blood; but we must remember that venous blood from an extremity was used, so that during the stage of absorption we should expect this to be lower than arterial blood, or venous blood from nonmuscular beds, which concentration would be the one reflected in the saliva. Thus it is probable that alcohol appears in saliva by a process of simple diffusion rather than active secretion. Since saliva is ordinarily swallowed, no alcohol would be lost from the body by this route. Even in an inveterate tobacco chewer one would not expect the volume of expectoration to be great enough to contain a significant amount of alcohol.

Feces.—There has been no adequate study of excretion of alcohol in the feces. This may be explained in part by the probable difficulty of applying the usual analytic methods for alcohol to this material, which might be expected to contain other volatile reducing substances. It is reasonable to suppose that feces contain about the same amount of alcohol per gram of water content as does blood, so that unless diarrhea were pronounced we should not expect more than 1% of the ingested alcohol at most to be eliminated by this channel. It is hardly conceivable that alcohol would reach the rectum before absorption, and even if it did it has been well demonstrated that it may be effectively absorbed from that site. Bacterial fermentation in the intestine, especially in herbivores, is productive of a small amount of alcohol; but this is no doubt rapidly absorbed, and metabolized.

All of the various secretions in the body probably approximate in their alcohol content that of the blood. It has been shown (15) in dogs that prostatic secretion contains approximately the same concentration of alcohol as does blood, while sperm showed values about half of this. The amount of these and other secretions which we have not considered specifically is not sufficient, however, to make any significant contribution to the elimination of alcohol from the body.

Thus we have seen that under ordinary circumstances, with large doses of alcohol approaching the tolerance of the animal body, approximately 10% of the ingested alcohol can be accounted for in the breath and the urine. With smaller doses, a proportionately smaller percentage will be eliminated by these routes. The remaining 90% or more is metabolized in the body, as we shall see in the next chapter.

REFERENCES

1. MILES, W. R., "The Comparative Concentrations of Alcohol in Human Blood and Urine at Intervals after Ingestion," *J. Pharmacol.*, **20**:265, 1922
2. JETTER, W. W., "Studies in Alcohol. I. The Diagnosis of Acute Alcoholic Intoxication by a Correlation of Clinical and Chemical Findings," *Am. J. Med. Sci.*, **196**:475, 1938
3. SOUTHGATE, H. W., and CARTER, G., "Excretion of Alcohol in the Urine as a Guide to Alcoholic Intoxication," *Brit. Med. J.*, **1**:463, 1926
4. SMITH, S., and STEWART, C. P., "Diagnosis of Drunkenness from the Excretion of Alcohol," *Brit. Med. J.*, **1**:89, January 1932
5. HAGGARD, H. W., and GREENBERG, L. A., "Studies in the Absorption, Distribution, and Elimination of Ethyl Alcohol. II. The Excretion of Alcohol in Urine and Expired Air, and the Distribution of Alcohol between Air and Water, Blood, and Urine," *J. Pharmacol.*, **52**:150, 1934
6. MARESCA, G., "Diuretic Action of Ethyl Alcohol in Chronic Alcoholics," *Rass. clin. terap. sci. affini*, **35**:270, 1936
7. MACNIDER, W. DEB., and DONNELLY, G. L., "Effect of the Prolonged Use of Ethyl Alcohol on Renal Function and Pathology in the Dog," *Proc. Soc. Exp. Biol. and Med.*, **29**:581, 1932
8. MURRAY, M. M., "The Diuretic Action of Alcohol and Its Relation to Pituitrin," *J. Physiol.*, **76**:379, 1932
9. LEVIN, E., "Effect of Alcohol on Blood Volume," *Rev. soc. argentina biol.*, **11**:277, 1935
10. HAGGARD, H. W., GREENBERG, L. A., CARROLL, R. P., and MILLER, D. P., "The Use of Urine in the Chemical Test for Intoxication: Possible Errors and Their Avoidance," *J. Am. Med. Assoc.*, **115**:1680, 1940
11. HARGER, R. N., LAMB, E. B., and HULPIEU, H. R., "A Rapid Chemical Test for Intoxication Employing Breath," *J. Am. Med. Assoc.*, **110**: 779, March 12, 1938
12. NYMAN, E., and PALMLOV, A., "The Elimination of Ethyl Alcohol in Sweat," *Skand. Arch. Physiol.*, **74**:155, August 1936
13. ABELS, J. C., "Determination of Ethyl Alcohol in Saliva," *Proc. Soc. Exp. Biol. and Med.*, **34**:504, 1936
14. FRIEDEMANN, T. E., MOTEL, W. G., and NECHELES, H., "The Excretion of Ingested Ethyl Alcohol in Saliva," *J. Lab. Clin. Med.*, **23**:1007, 1938
15. FARRELL, J. I., "The Secretion of Alcohol by the Genital Tract," *J. Urol.*, **40**:62, 1938

CHAPTER III

COMBUSTION

We have seen that not more than 10% of ingested alcohol is excreted, leaving at least 90% to be burned in the body. This combustion of ethyl alcohol proceeds eventually to the production of carbon dioxide and water, with the production of approximately 7 calories per gram of alcohol burned. The exact amount of alcohol that can be burned daily by a man has never been experimentally determined, although we are all familiar with the estimates given by alcohol addicts, not infrequently ranging upward from a quart of whisky. It seems likely that such estimates are in the nature of boasting, as Widmark has estimated (1) that a man of 70 kg. should be able to metabolize a maximum of 170 gm. of alcohol daily, equal to but a pint of 90-proof whisky. There is no doubt that more than this amount may be ingested in a 24-hour period, with its elimination extending well into the next day; but it is most unlikely that such a rate of consumption could be continued without interruption for any period without a lethal outcome. As a matter of fact, the combination of the anesthetic and the emetic effects of alcohol operate to limit its intake quite effectively.

Energy derived from alcohol.—The amount of energy made available by 170 gm. of alcohol would be 1,190 calories, a very considerable proportion of the basal metabolic requirement. In confirmation of the validity of Widmark's estimate of maximal alcohol consumption is the direct appraisal of the percentage of the energy requirement in man that is covered by alcohol after a single small dose. Carpenter (2) gave a dose of 10 cc. of alcohol to a man, and determined the length of time alcohol could be detected in the expired air, using this as an index of the length of time required for its oxidation. At the same time the oxygen consumption and carbon dioxide production was measured, allowing the investigators to calculate the amount of energy liberated and the amount of alcohol burned, and from this the percentage of the energy derived from alcohol, which was 49 to 75% of the total. Since the same author showed that the alcohol caused no significant increase in the metabolic rate, it is obvious that we cannot greatly increase Widmark's maximum estimate without turning up with an excess of energy on our hands, and thus must accept it as a close approximation of the actual maximum, statements of alcoholics notwithstanding.

Rate of combustion and temperature.—In poikilothermic animals, when the total metabolism is decreased by low environmental temperature, alcohol combustion may account for up to 90% of heat production. Nicloux (3, 4) administered alcohol in known dosage subcutaneously to frogs, then placed them in a jar from which the urine and expired air could be obtained for alcohol analysis. At the end of 24 hours the frogs were sacrificed and the alcohol remaining in their bodies was determined. Since oxygen consumption was also followed, it was possible to determine the percentage of the energy derived from alcohol. The procedure was carried out at environmental temperatures of from 1° to 29° C., the range compatible with life in the frog under the experimental conditions. At 1° C. 18% of the energy was provided by alcohol, at 29° 86%. From the data so obtained Nicloux determined that combustion of alcohol in the frog conforms to Van't Hoff's coefficient for chemical reactions; that is, there is a doubling of the rate of alcohol metabolism for a rise of 10° C., the actual coefficient for the range from 1° to 29° C. being 1.97. LeBreton (5) later found that in fasted frogs and turtles, kept in the dark at an environmental temperature of 10° C., alcohol accounted for 90% of the total energy exchange. Thus it is obvious that in the cold-blooded animal alcohol is capable of providing almost the total energy requirement. Whether or not the small percentage that cannot be so derived indicates that alcohol cannot be utilized for certain metabolic functions has not been experimentally demonstrated.

Alcohol combustion in vitro.—The site of oxidation of alcohol in the body has been definitely known for only a few years, and even now our knowledge in this regard is incomplete. That alcohol can be burned in vitro by liver tissue has long been known. Battelli and Stern (6) in 1909 found this to be true for horse liver. They minced the tissue, which they suspended in 0.1% ammonia containing small concentrations of alcohol of known amount, replaced the air in the flask with oxygen, and agitated it for a period at 37 degrees. Alcohol disappeared at the rate of 150–200 mgm. per 100 gm. of liver; oxygen was used up, but no carbon dioxide was produced. The end product of the reaction was acetic acid. The muscle of the horse or steer was devoid of this property, which was found in aqueous or acetone extracts of beef or horse liver, but not of human liver. If we assume the liver in man to be equal to 3% of the body weight, alcohol metabolized at the rate shown by these authors in the horse in vitro would account for about 5 gm. per hour, approximately 75% of the amount actually metabolized in the intact man, indicating that the liver is at least a very important organ in the metabolism of alcohol. More recently this oxidation of alcohol in vitro by liver tissue has been confirmed by a number of investigators, among them LeBreton (7), Newman, Cutting, and Tainter (8), and Leloir and Munoz (9). All investigators are agreed that the end product of alcohol metabolism in the liver in vitro is acetic acid, and that liver tissue is incapable of carrying the process further, as no carbon dioxide is produced. The process might better be termed a dehydrogenation, in that it is thought (7) that the enzyme, called alcohol dehydrase, is capable of removing hydrogen from two molecules of alcohol and that these go on to form one molecule of acetic acid and one molecule of alcohol.

The amount of alcohol metabolized per hour by each gram of liver in vitro is not sufficient to account for the rate of disappearance of alcohol in the intact animal; but it is of such magnitude, considering the artificial conditions under which it takes place, as to be compatible with the conception that the liver is the sole site of the primary oxidation of alcohol. Thus LeBreton found (7) that when the liver was suspended in defibrinated blood, alcohol was metabolized at a rate of 2 gm. per kilogram of liver—very closely in accord with the earlier work of Battelli and Stern, and a rather close approach to the rate prevailing in the intact animal.

The enzyme responsible for this oxidation, or perhaps better, dehydrogenation, is present in water or acetone extracts; and a potent dried enzyme, not sensitive to cyanide, has been prepared (10).

Combustion in perfused organs.—As the next step in the elucidation of the site of metabolism of alcohol, Feissinger *et al.* (11) in 1936 demonstrated that the perfused liver was capable of metabolizing alcohol. They artificially perfused dog livers with defibrinated dog blood, either through the portal vein alone or through both the portal vein and the hepatic artery simultaneously, at a rate of flow of from 300 to 600 cc. per kilogram of liver per minute. Alcohol in the amount of 1.5 to 2.0 gm. per liter was added to the perfusion fluid. The alcohol concentration of the fluid decreased rapidly for a short time, during which presumably equilibrium was being established with the liver tissue, and then fell more slowly at a constant rate characteristic of the metabolism of alcohol in the intact organism. There were burned 1.35 gm. of alcohol per kilogram of liver per hour—a figure comparable to that obtained in the in vitro experiments. The addition of KCN in a concentration of 0.2 to 0.3 gm. per liter stopped the alcohol oxidation, which was partly restored by sodium hyposulphite 1.0 to 2.0 gm. per liter. Thus it was demonstrated that the isolated perfused liver of the dog was able to burn alcohol at a rate somewhat less than half that which prevails in the intact dog, definitely proving that the liver, if not actually responsible for the primary oxidation of all the alcohol, at least burns much more than its share on a weight basis.

This work was confirmed the next year by Lundsgaard (12) in cats. His technic was essentially similar to that of the French workers. He chose the cat rather than the dog because in this animal it is much more feasible to maintain a constant perfusion flow without changes in the portal pressure than is the case in the dog. He also measured oxygen uptake. Alcohol was found to disappear from the perfusion fluid at a constant rate, which was approximately 60% that prevailing in the intact cat. The investigator felt that this was about what one would expect, under the somewhat unfavorable conditions of the experimental situation, if the liver were the sole site of alcohol oxidation. Sufficient oxygen was not consumed to carry the oxidation to completion, and he felt that it probably went only as far as acetic acid. He also carried out the perfusion of the hind limbs of cats in the same manner, and found that there was no disappearance of alcohol in such preparations, indicating that muscle was unable to initiate the oxidation of alcohol, a finding in keeping with the work in vitro. His conclusions were that the primary step or steps in the oxidation of alcohol take place solely in the liver.

Having had an opportunity of observing Lundsgaard's work in his laboratory, Newman *et al.* (13) repeated and confirmed it. They found that in the isolated, perfused cat liver, using defibrinated cat blood oxygenated by bubbling a stream of oxygen slowly through it in a tall cylinder, the oxygen consumption and carbon dioxide production, as measured with the Van Slyke apparatus, remained essentially constant for a period of two hours. Lactic acid concentration fell rapidly from a high initial value, no doubt due to its rapid production in the exsanguination of the cats from which the perfusion fluid was obtained, to a value around 75 mgm.%, after which the fall was much slower. Blood sugar fell from an initial value of around 150 mgm.% to about half that value at the end of the two hours, the fall being fairly constant. The glycogen content of the liver decreased slightly less than 25%. When alcohol was added to the perfusion fluid in a quantity sufficient to achieve a concentration of approximately 300 mgm.%, the changes in the various metabolites were somewhat different from what they were in control perfusions. The alcohol concentration fell at an essentially constant rate. There was a decrease in both carbon dioxide production and oxygen consumption. The glycogen content of the liver decreased to a significantly greater extent than in the controls, while the blood lactic acid increased rather than decreased. All of these changes suggest a depression of the metabolic processes of the liver, and indicate thus a toxic action of alcohol on liver function. That alcohol is burned in preference to glucose is indicated by the fact that the blood sugar concentration fell much less rapidly than in the controls. In summary, the experiments showed that alcohol is metabolized in the liver, at the expense of the burning of glucose, and that this metabolism of alcohol is accompanied by a decrease in oxygen consumption and carbon dioxide production, a reduction of the glycogen store, and an increase in blood lactic acid concentration, all indicating a toxic action of alcohol on the liver.

Rate of combustion in perfused liver.—In all the perfusion work it was apparent that the rate at which alcohol disappeared was not proportional to the concentration present, but rather that it proceeded at an essentially constant rate regardless of concentration. This was equally true in the experiments concerning the combustion of alcohol by liver in vitro, and this we shall see also prevails in a somewhat restricted sense in the intact animal. It would seem that the efficiency of the enzyme system in the liver is the governing factor in the rate of alcohol metabolism. Thus we should expect this rate of metabolism to be resistant to change from external factors—an expectation that is borne out in practice.

Rate of combustion and amount of liver tissue.—That the rate of alcohol metabolism is intimately related to the amount of functional liver tissue has been shown by a number of investigators, both experimentally in animals and in man with clinical disease of the liver. Chapheau (14) determined the curve of blood alcohol in control rabbits receiving 2 cc. of alcohol per kilogram body weight by stomach tube. He analyzed blood samples taken at intervals of 2, 5, and 7 hours after ingestion by the method of Nicloux. Complete abolition of kidney function brought about by the administration of 5 to 6 mgm. of uranium nitrate did not in any way alter the blood alcohol curve, indicating the nonparticipation of the kidneys in the metabolism of alcohol. When 1 cc. of phosphorated oil was given on two successive days to produce liver damage, the rate of fall of blood alcohol was much reduced over that of the controls, indicating the liver has an important role in alcohol oxidation. This was confirmed by Broggi (15), who found the same slow decline of the blood alcohol concentration after damage to the liver with chloroform. He states that similar curves are seen in alcohol addicts and patients with liver disease, and suggests the use of the blood alcohol curve as a test of liver function. Erwteman and Heeres (16) found that in rabbits chronically poisoned by phosphorus in oil the blood alcohol curve showed a higher maximum than the controls, followed by an initial sharp drop and then a plateau or slight rise. Similar curves were demonstrated after the oral administration of a test dose of one-fifth gram alcohol per kilogram body weight in patients suffering from carcinoma with liver metastases and in cirrhosis. In catarrhal jaundice and cholelithiasis the maximum concentration was higher than normal, but the period of decline was essentially the same as in the controls. Evidently in these disorders alcohol metabolism is not disturbed, although other functions of the liver are. The authors postulate a normal blood alcohol curve after one-fifth gram of alcohol per kilogram as follows: The "resting value," or so-called normal blood alcohol without ingestion of alcohol, varies from 2 to 9 mgm.%. The summit of the blood alcohol curve should be from 15.5 to 19.0 mgm.% and should occur 30 minutes after ingestion. The descent should be in a straight line at a rate in excess of 13 mgm.% in 2½ hours. They propose the use of this procedure as a test of liver function.

The possible objection may be raised that, since the alcohol is given by mouth, factors influencing the rate of absorption may alter the curve and lead to errors in interpretation. Administration of the alcohol intravenously would seem to be preferable, and when so administered it would seem reasonable to expect the alcohol tolerance curve to be an accurate test of the ability of the liver to metabolize alcohol. Unfortunately, it tests but one function of the liver, in common with so many of the tests ordinarily used. How well its results correlate with pathological findings is yet to be determined, but warrants competent investigation.

Site of alcohol metabolism.—Mirsky and Nelson (17) found that after evisceration of rabbits there was no apparent fall of blood alcohol concentration, a finding that we had observed independently in the dog some years previously (18). This is in confirmation of the work of Lundsgaard (12) showing lack of utilization of alcohol by muscle. Mirsky and Nelson also demonstrated that partial removal of the liver of a rabbit slowed the rate of alcohol metabolism and that, moreover, this slowing was proportional to the amount of liver removed. This evidence supports the use of alcohol tolerance as a liver-function test; but it must still be borne in mind that the liver has many functions, and that the presence or absence of the ability to metabolize alcohol has not been proved to bear any definite relationship to the presence or absence of these various other functions. It does, however, seem a reliable index of the amount of liver tissue present. These authors also confirmed the slowing of alcohol metabolism after chloroform inhalation in the rabbit. They found that anesthesia produced by chloroform for a 15-minute period daily for 5 days slowed the rate of fall of blood alcohol by 40%. After an interval of 12 days, the rate had returned to normal, showing the process to be a reversible one.

It is also significant that the two agents which we shall see are generally accepted as effective in accelerating alcohol metabolism, insulin and amino acids, are intimately associated with liver function. Thus it is seen that the bulk of experimental evidence points to the liver as the sole site of the initial process involved in the oxidation of alcohol.

Concentration and rate of metabolism.—One of the problems of alcohol metabolism over which the greatest controversy has raged is that of the relationship between the rate of alcohol metabolism and the concentration of alcohol in the body. This had received little consideration before the fundamental work of Mellanby in 1919 (19). Experiments on 4 dogs given alcohol by stomach tube in doses of from 1 to 4 cc. per kilogram body weight demonstrated in every case that after a maximum blood concentration was achieved the rate of fall of blood alcohol concentration remained constant as long as alcohol was demonstrable in the blood. To quote: "After reaching a maximum, the Curve A descends in a straight line to the abscissa. This means that the rate of oxidation is constant throughout the whole period, and this is the case in spite of the fact that the amount of alcohol in the body is getting progressively less. The interpretation of this fact is therefore that, whatever the amount of alcohol in the body, the rate of oxidation is constant, or, in other words, the rate of oxidation of alcohol is independent of the amount drunk." Nicloux and Widmark confirmed this aspect of Mellanby's work, and on the basis of this constancy of metabolism Widmark (20) worked out his calculation of the factors r and β as noted in a preceding chapter.

This was the generally accepted concept when, in 1934, Haggard and Greenberg (21) presented findings diametrically in opposition. They administered alcohol intravenously to dogs as a 30% solution in normal saline, the dosage varying from 2.0 to 4.5 gm. per kilogram body weight, and followed the concentration in the arterial blood for a period of 11 hours. The curves so obtained were exponential in character, rather than linear. Their conclusions were, to quote: "1. Contrary to the generally accepted belief, rate of alcohol oxidation is not constant regardless of the amount present in the body. On the contrary the rate of oxidation is proportional to the amount of alcohol present in the body. 2. Each hour the amount of alcohol present is diminished by a uniform per cent. In 4 dogs studied the individual percentage rates ranged from 21.1 to 15.9 with an average of 17.6%." They explained the results of the previous workers who had administered alcohol by mouth as being due to prolonged absorption of alcohol from the gastrointestinal tract, resulting in an appearance of the blood alcohol curve which conveyed the false impression of a constant rate of metabolism. This explanation could hardly account for the previously published straight-line curves of Gabbe in 1917 (22) and Mehrtens and Newman in 1933 (23). As a matter of fact, search of the literature fails to reveal any curves of blood alcohol concentration after a single dose by any route which resemble the exponential curves presented by Haggard and Greenberg, as can be seen from the representative reproductions shown in Figures 5 and 6. When, after a lapse of some six years, we find the authors again presenting curves of blood alcohol, this time in the rat (24) after administration of alcohol into the duodenum, the curves have the orthodox straight-line form, without any explanation of the discrepancy of these and the previous curves. The closest we can come to such an explanation has been well put by Eggleton (25): "The cause of the wide variation of results of Haggard and Greenberg from those of other workers is obscure."

The work of Haggard and Greenberg was not, however, without value, for it was effective in stimulating further research into the effect of dosage on the rate of alcohol metabolism. Newman and Cutting (26) were the first to accept the challenge. Incidental to other investigations, Newman had followed the blood alcohol concentration after intravenous injection of from 0.5 to 1.5 cc. of alcohol per kilogram in 20 human subjects, and felt that their consistent linear form supported the work of Mellanby. Since the conflicting results of Haggard and Greenberg were obtained by similar experimental methods, excepting the method of alcohol analysis, another approach to the problem seemed indi-

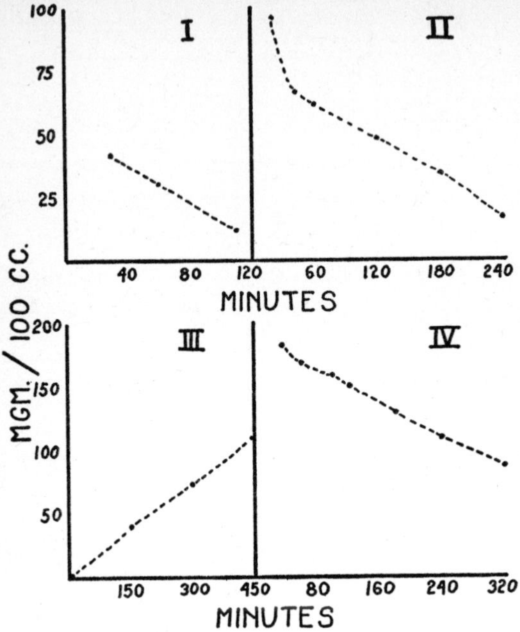

FIG. 5.—Blood alcohol concentration after a single dose of alcohol. I. Intravenous injection of 0.3 gm. per kilogram in man (Gabbe, 1917). II. Intravenous injection of 0.6 cc. per kilogram in man (Fleming and Reynolds, 1935). III. Intravenous injection of 1.0 gm. per kilogram in the dog (Mirsky and Nelson, 1939). IV. Intravenous injection of 1.5 gm. per kilogram in the rabbit (LeBreton, 1935).

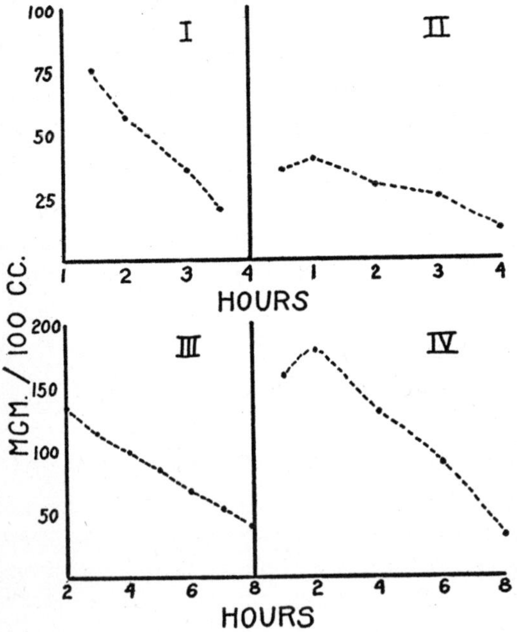

FIG. 6.—Blood alcohol concentration after a single dose of alcohol. I. Introduction of 1.0 gm. per kilogram into the duodenum of a dog (Haggard and Greenberg, 1940). II. Ingestion of 0.6 cc. per kilogram in man (Blotner, 1939). III. Urine alcohol concentration after ingestion of 216 cc. of whisky in man (Smith and Stewart, 1932). IV. Ingestion of 2.0 cc. per kilogram in man (Jetter, 1938).

cated. They therefore determined, in man, the amount of alcohol required per hour to maintain the alcohol concentration of the blood at different levels, on the reasonable assumption that if this were constant it would definitely show the metabolic rate of alcohol not to be related to the concentration of alcohol in the blood. A preliminary injection of 1.0 cc. per kilogram was given to each of two subjects in order to learn approximately how much alcohol they were capable of metabolizing hourly. Subsequently each was given an initial injection of ⅓ cc. per kilogram, and, after an interval for equilibration, a slow intravenous infusion at the previously calculated rate was continued for a period of 5 hours. Blood alcohol determinations showed these amounts to be capable of maintaining the level constant over this period. On a subsequent occasion an initial dose of 1.0 cc. per kilogram was given to each subject, and continuous infusion with the same dosage per hour was carried out. Again, in spite of the higher blood alcohol concentrations, the level remained constant. From this the authors concluded that "The amount of alcohol per unit time required to maintain the blood alcohol of an individual at a given concentration is constant, and independent of the height of the blood alcohol, at least within the limits of this investigation, 15 to 94 mgm. per 100 cc." The average maintenance dose per hour they found to be .174 cc. per kilogram, slightly less than the .185 cc. per kilogram found by Mellanby in the dog. This work could be interpreted only as confirming that of the earlier workers and effectively controverting that of Haggard and Greenberg.

Since 1935 there have been a number of studies to support the constant-rate thesis. Fleming and coworkers (27, 28) gave 0.6 cc. of alcohol to many human subjects intravenously, and all of their cases showed a constant rate of fall. Jetter (29) gave doses from 1 to 2 cc. per kilogram to fasting men, and his curves have the form of a straight line after absorption was complete and equilibrium established. The data secured by Goldfarb, Bowman, and Parker on their control group in a study of the glucose and insulin on acute alcoholism (30) are pertinent: They took an initial sample of blood on 26 alcoholics brought into the hospital, and another sample 2 hours later. From these two samples, analyzed for alcohol, they were able to state the fall of the blood alcohol concentration in 2 hours, which for the whole group averaged 50 mgm.%. They then separated the subjects into two groups, those having an initial blood alcohol concentration above 300 mgm.% being called severely intoxicated and those with lower concentrations moderately intoxicated. The rate of fall of blood alcohol was 53 mgm.% in the former, and 48 mgm.% in the latter group—hardly a significant difference, in spite of the fact that the average blood concentrations were quite divergent.

Further confirmatory evidence for the constant rate comes from Haggard and Greenberg (24) themselves. In work designed to investigate the effect of amino acids on alcohol metabolism, they administered a single dose of 2 gm. per kilogram and followed the blood alcohol concentration for 5 hours, at which time it had fallen to 75 mgm.%. They then gave the same dose, only this time slowly and constantly spread over the 5-hour period, with the result that at the end of the period the blood alcohol concentration had reached approximately the same point as with the single dose, indicating the same amount of unburned alcohol with either system of administration. When it is considered that the average blood alcohol concentration with the single dose was several times that with the continuous, and that the same amount of alcohol was burned in both cases, it is apparent that this is further evidence in favor of a constant rate of metabolism.

The majority of these studies indicating a constant rate of alcohol metabolism were based on the assumption that the rate of alcohol metabolism could be accurately gauged from the rate of fall of blood alcohol concentration. LeBreton (31) has done some work bearing directly on this point. She administered alcohol intravenously and intraperitoneally to rats and rabbits, determined the blood alcohol concentration at intervals thereafter, and then sacrificed the animals and determined the amount of alcohol remaining in the carcass. In rabbits, the factor *r* of Widmark varied widely between .72 and 1.0, and the factor β indicative of rate of metabolism also varied. In the rat *r* was constant at 0.8, and β was also constant in the individual. In accord with these results, the rate of metabolism as determined by Widmark's formula from the blood alcohol curve checked well with that determined directly by difference between the amount of alcohol administered and the amount recovered from the carcass after an interval in the case of the rat; but this was not so in the case of the rabbit. From this she concluded that the rate of alcohol metabolism could be validly estimated from the blood alcohol curve in the rat but not in the rabbit. In a later paper (32) she reported giving 1.5 gm. per kilogram orally, intraperitoneally, and intravenously to rabbits, after which she followed the blood alcohol concentration for 5 hours, and then sacrificed the animals and assayed the carcasses. The two methods checked only after intravenous injection and not after oral or intraperitoneal injection, where the discrepancies amounted to as much as 15%. This work was complicated by the simultaneous administration of peptone, alanine, and glucose for some purpose not mentioned and evidently connected with other work she was doing; hence it is difficult to evaluate properly. Another paper reported at the same time (33) dealt with the effect of concentration on the rate of alcohol metabolism. Here she determined the rate of metabolism directly by analysis of the whole animal at an interval after the administration of varying doses of alcohol, the range being from 0.5 to 2.5 gm. per kilogram. She concluded that while this range of dosage had no effect on the rate of metabolism in the rat and mouse, the guinea pig, cock, and rabbit showed a faster metabolism with the higher doses. She expressed the rate of metabolism in milligrams per kilogram per hour, which she called the Coefficient of Ethyloxidation, or C.E.O. A valid criticism of this work lay in the small number of animals, there being but 4 guinea pigs, 4 cocks, and 10 rabbits. Thus there was more difference in C.E.O. among rabbits at the same dose than between those at different doses. For instance, after 1.9 gm. per kilogram one rabbit had a C.E.O. of 320, while another on the smaller dose of 1.5 gm. per kilogram had a slower rate of 265. However, another at 1.5 gm. per kilogram had a rate of 121, a difference far greater than that between the two doses. Incidentally, in the previous paper there is a curve of blood alcohol in a rabbit which is definitely linear, supporting the thesis that in this animal too the rate of alcohol metabolism is constant.

Although over the relatively small range of concentrations of blood alcohol investigated in man, Newman and his coworkers (26) found the rate of alcohol metabolism to be essentially constant, when larger doses were given to animals it was at once apparent that this generalization could not be applied over the whole range of concentrations of alcohol compatible with life. As a matter of fact, on re-examination of the original curves of Mellanby (19) it is readily apparent that although the curves as plotted in his Figure I (which represents the blood alcohol concentrations following doses of 55, 50, 30, and 20 cc. in a dog of 13 kgm.) have an essentially linear form in the post-absorptive phase, when we compare the slope of those at low concentrations with those at high the latter are definitely steeper. Thus with the 50 cc. dose we find that (these values are scaled from the figure) from 2½ to 6 hours after administration the blood alcohol concentration falls from 421 to 322 mgm.%, a drop of 99, while with the 20 cc. dose in the same period the drop is from 133 to 74, or 59. Thus there was evidently more alcohol burned per hour with the higher dose than with the lower. This is not, however, in the direct proportionality proposed by Haggard and Greenberg, since the higher rate is but 68% greater than the lower, while the average blood alcohol concentration with the larger dose was 372 mgm.% against 103 mgm.% for the smaller, a ratio of almost four to one.

In order to investigate this problem, Newman, Lehman, and Cutting (34) administered a wide range of doses of alcohol, from 1 to 6 cc. per kilogram, to dogs by the intravenous route, and followed the blood alcohol concentration until it fell to the base line. From the slope of the blood alcohol curve the rate of metabolism was calculated by Widmark's method. It was obvious that the tendency apparent in Mellanby's curves was borne out by the data obtained, the rate of metabolism being definitely more rapid with the higher doses. Interestingly, the authors calculated that for an increase of 100% in the blood alcohol concentration there was an increase of approximately 17% in the rate of metabolism, which is almost identical with the 68% change for an increase of 360% in concentration calculated from Mellanby's curves.

Strikingly enough, in spite of the more rapid fall with high dosage, the curves at all doses showed a straight-line fall; and this is true equally of those of Mellanby. Thus the steepness of the curve in the zone from 100 to 0 mgm.% after a 6 cc. per kilogram dose is considerably greater than that in the same zone after a 1 cc. dose. In confirmation of this, it was shown that if a large dose was given, and when the blood alcohol concentration had almost fallen to zero a second dose of 1 cc. per kilogram administered, the rate of fall after this second dose was characteristic of that after a large dose, and much faster than that after a 1 cc. dose without a previous large one. The authors are unable to explain this apparent "conditioning" of the rate of alcohol metabolism by the highest concentration reached. They conclude: "it seems evident that the rate at which alcohol disappears from the blood in a given dog remains constant throughout, although this rate is dependent to some extent on the amount of alcohol administered." They felt that this dependence on dose was not of sufficient magnitude to invalidate the work of Widmark.

Here the situation rested until the publication of the researches of Eggleton (35, 25). Working with cats anesthetized with nembutal, which she felt had a negligible effect on the rate of alcohol metabolism, she administered the alcohol intravenously. The alcohol concentration of the carotid arterial blood was determined at intervals by the method of Newman (36) modified in several details to give it a higher degree of accuracy. The same method was used for the determination of tissue alcohol, a trichloracetic acid filtrate of the minced tissues being used. She found under these experimental conditions that the factor *r* of Widmark was constant in the cat at all intervals after injection and on different occasions. She gave a single intravenous injection of alcohol to a cat, and determined the rate of metabolism by Widmark's method. Constant intravenous infusion of alcohol at this rate, in much the same manner as that employed earlier by Newman and Cutting, was effective in maintaining the blood alcohol concentration constant for a period of three hours. From this she concludes that in the cat Widmark's method of determining rate of alcohol metabolism from the blood alcohol curve is valid, at least when the alcohol is administered intravenously.

She then determined the rate of metabolism in cats after two doses of different size, the small dose being given first, followed by the larger dose when the blood alcohol concentration had dropped almost to zero. Under these conditions it was obvious that the higher doses carried with them a more rapid rate of metabolism, for with blood alcohol concentrations above 20 mgm.% an increase of 100 mgm.% in blood alcohol entailed on the average an increase in metabolic rate of 30%. This is fairly well in line with the findings of Newman *et al.* and with the calculated differences from Mellanby's data. She then followed the blood alcohol concentration in the cat over a long period following a single injection, so that the rate of fall in the early hours after the injection could be compared with that in the later hours when the blood alcohol concentration was much lower. Here we see a discrepancy with previous work, as there was a gradual reduction of the rate of metabolism with decreasing concentration of alcohol, although not by any means the 17%

each hour postulated by Haggard and Greenberg, but rather of the same order of magnitude as that shown with the large-and-small-dose investigation. In this regard Eggleton's work is not in agreement with that of Mellanby or Newman *et al.* It must be remembered, however, that there is a species difference, since the latter investigators employed the dog rather than the cat. That this may be an explanation is indicated by the fact that Eggleton reported the results of measurement of the metabolic rate over a long period after a single injection in one dog, and here the difference in rate at different intervals after the injection is significantly less than in the case of the cats. In fact, from 6 to 12 hours after the injection the rate of fall was 90 mgm. per kilogram per hour, while from 12 to 16 hours it was 84 mgm. per kilogram per hour—probably not a significant difference.

Eggleton then resorted to a procedure rather similar to that employed by Newman and Cutting in man. In each of two cats, a slow constant infusion of alcohol was given over a period of about three hours, during which the blood alcohol concentration rose slowly, in one case to about 7 mgm.% and in the other to about 22 mgm.%. A single large injection of alcohol was then given sufficient to raise the blood alcohol concentration above 300 mgm.%, and after about an hour for equilibration constant slow infusion at the same rate as at first was started and maintained for a little over three hours, with a resultant fall in blood alcohol concentration in both cases. This work can only be interpreted as indicating an increased rate of metabolism at higher concentrations. If we can carry these results over to man, it would indicate that the constancy of rate shown by Newman and Cutting for the range of concentration up to 100 mgm.% does not hold for higher concentrations—a thesis in accord with the later work of Newman, Lehman, and Cutting in dogs. In connection with the finding of the latter workers of a rapid rate of metabolism of a small dose administered just before the blood alcohol had fallen to zero subsequent to a large dose, it would be of interest to repeat the experiment of Eggleton in the reverse direction, maintaining the blood alcohol concentration constant with a slow infusion at say 300 mgm.%, then allowing it to fall to around 50 mgm.%, and again starting the slow infusion at the some rate as at first. Should the blood alcohol remain constant, it would be excellent evidence of the "conditioning" of the rate of metabolism by the highest concentration of blood alcohol.

While the rate of metabolism varied considerably from cat to cat, Eggleton found that if liver weight rather than body weight or body surface were considered, the variation disappeared to a considerable degree, although there still remained an appreciable range. This is further evidence supporting the liver as the governing factor in alcohol metabolism.

Species differences.—That there is a species difference both in the factor r of Widmark, which is the mean alcohol concentration of the whole body expressed as a fraction of the concentration in the blood, and in the rate of metabolism of alcohol has been well established. Thus Widmark found (20) that r for dogs was .75, for man .68. Newman and Lehman determined r and β, which is the rate of alcohol metabolism expressed in milligrams per gram per minute, in a variety of species at varying blood alcohol concentrations. The technic of Widmark was varied only by administering the alcohol intravenously rather than orally, thus eliminating possibility of variations in absorption influencing the results. A sufficient period was allowed to elapse after the injection to insure equilibrium being established between the blood and tissues before the first blood sample was taken. Blood samples from dogs, cats, and men were obtained from the peripheral veins of an extremity, while with rabbits and pigeons cardiac puncture was employed and with chickens puncture of the comb. The factors r and β were determined for each species after injection of two different doses, to test the constancy of these factors at widely divergent blood alcohol concentrations. The factor r was found to be constant regardless of dose in man, the dog, the cat, and the pigeon, while in the rabbit and the chicken this was not so, in the former animal it being larger with the small dose and in the latter larger with the large dose. As a matter of fact, in both the rabbit and the chicken the factor *r* at times exceeds unity, indicating a greater concentration in the body as a whole than exists in the blood stream. This can mean one of two things: either there is a very rapid initial destruction of a considerable amount of alcohol by these species, or they are capable of storing alcohol in their tissues in greater concentration than it exists in the circulation. Neither of these concepts is in accord with our knowledge of the metabolism of alcohol. The former, that involving an initial rapid destruction of alcohol, is in keeping with the finding by LeBreton (33, 38) that the rate of alcohol metabolism in these two species was greater at high than at low concentrations of alcohol. Newman and Lehman could not confirm this finding, as their work showed the rate of fall of blood alcohol concentration to be the same after widely divergent doses. It must be remembered, however, that they assessed the rate of metabolism from the blood alcohol curve, in which the initial destruction of a considerable amount of alcohol would not be apparent, while LeBreton determined the actual amount of alcohol which disappeared from the body by analysis of the carcass. Thus the discrepancy between the results of Newman and Lehman and of LeBreton may well be explained by an initial very high rate of destruction of alcohol in the rabbit and the chicken, followed by oxidation at the orthodox constant rate. In what manner this initial destruction is accomplished we have not even a conjecture to offer, but it seems to be the only hypothesis that fits all the facts.

Rate of metabolism and size of animal.—Newman and Lehman found the rate of metabolism of alcohol to increase in general as the size of the animal decreased. Thus the rabbit had a higher rate than the cat, the cat a higher rate than the dog, the dog a higher rate than man. On the other hand, in the birds the chicken had a higher rate than the much smaller pigeon—an observation in accord with that of LeBreton, Nicloux, and Shaeffer (39). These authors felt that the rate of alcohol metabolism was proportional to the basal metabolic rate of the animal. They gave 1.5 gm. of alcohol per kilogram intraperitoneally to a variety of animals and determined the rate of alcohol metabolism by analyzing the whole animal after an interval. The C.E.O. for the various species was as follows: mouse, 550; rat, 270; guinea pig, 209; rabbit, 176; pigeon, 287; and chicken, 308. The somewhat higher rate of metabolism in birds may be due in part to their higher body temperature, since we have seen that in cold-blooded animals the metabolism of alcohol is subject to Van't Hoff's coefficient for chemical reactions. This same relationship to basal metabolism can be seen in the evolution of the rate of alcohol metabolism with age and growth. LeBreton (38) found that in the white rat when the C.E.O. is determined during growth it falls from 628 at 30 days of age to 274 at 120 days, during which time the basal metabolic rate falls by an approximately equal percentage from 10 to 4 calories per kilogram per hour. Thus the percentage of the basal requirement supplied by alcohol remains at approximately 50% at all ages. In the white leghorn cock, however, there is little change in the C.E.O. from 6 days to 2 years of age, with the result that alcohol provides more and more of the energy requirement up to 82% in the adult bird. Here again we have a difference in the mechanism of alcohol metabolism between the chicken and the rat, alcohol providing a constant percentage of the basal energy requirement in the rat, while in the chicken the percentage increases as the basal rate decreases with age. Again we are unaware of the significance of this species difference.

Because of this relationship between basal metabolic rate and rate of alcohol metabolism, it is of interest to investigate the action of agents known to be effective in altering the basal metabolic rate on the speed of combustion of alcohol. This has been done, the agents investigated being thyroid substance or thyroxin, dinitrophenol, and hyperpyrexia.

Thyroid.—Widmark (40) and Harger and Hulpieu (41) administered thyroxin to dogs without in any significant way altering their rate of alcohol metabolism. Newman administered alcohol intravenously to a patient with hypothyroidism and determined the rate of metabolism. Thyroid substance was then given in dosage effective in raising the basal metabolic rate to normal, and another test dose of alcohol was administered. There was no significant change in the rate of alcohol metabolism before and after thyroid medication, in spite of the change in basal metabolic rate. This evidence indicates that the administration of thyroid substance or thyroxin, in man and the dog, either normal or suffering from thyroid deficiency, is not effective in significantly increasing the rate of metabolism of alcohol, even though the basal metabolic rate be considerably increased.

Dinitrophenol.—It is well known that the administration of dinitrophenol or dinitrocresol in adequate dosage is effective in increasing the basal metabolic rate. The effect of this agent on the oxidation of alcohol by rat liver in vitro was investigated by Newman, Cutting, and Tainter (8). Male white rats of from 250 to 300 gm. were killed by a blow on the head and decapitated. The liver was immediately removed and sections 0.5 mm. in thickness were prepared. Next, 300 mgm. of the liver slices were placed in a 25 cc. Erlenmeyer flask, 3 cc. of 0.1% alcohol in phosphate buffer of pH 7.4 and 0.3 cc. of the appropriate dilution of dinitrophenol were added, and the air was displaced by oxygen. Each determination was run in duplicate, with duplicate controls from the same liver, which differed only in the absence of the dinitrophenol. The flasks were agitated for two hours in an incubator at 37° C. Oxidation was stopped by placing them in ice water, and the alcohol remaining was determined. Concentrations of dinitrophenol of from 1:5,000,000 to 1:20,000,000 caused a slight but consistent increase in alcohol consumption, while higher concentrations depressed alcohol oxidation. These effects occurred at the same concentrations, and were of about the same order of magnitude, as found by McCord for oxygen consumption in a medium of the same pH. In confirmation of this work, Leloir and Munoz (9), using a rather similar method, found that dinitrophenol in a concentration of $1.1 \times 10^{-5}M$ increased the rate of alcohol metabolism, while higher concentrations decreased it. Thus it is evident that dinitrophenol has some slight action directly on the liver to increase the rate of alcohol combustion, at least in the rat.

This work in vitro had been preceded by the demonstration in dogs of an increased rate of fall of blood alcohol after administration of dinitrophenol and dinitrocresol. Widmark (42) gave an 18.3 kg. dog 31.6 gm. of alcohol by stomach tube. He followed the blood alcohol concentration for 255 minutes, at the end of which time 10 mgm. per kilogram of dinitrophenol were given by mouth. The body temperature rose to 39.3° C., and the metabolic rate more than doubled. A similar increase in rate of alcohol metabolism was produced by 200 mgm. of dinitrocresol in the same dog. The investigator was unable to decide whether the increase in alcohol metabolism was due to a direct action of the increased basal metabolism, to the fever, or to the hyperventilation produced.

Harger and Hulpieu (41) gave alcohol to dogs by stomach tube in doses from 1.5 to 3.0 gm. per kilogram and determined the blood alcohol concentration at intervals over a twelve-hour period. They state that the rate of disappearance of alcohol from the blood was greatly increased by doses of 7.5 to 15 mgm. per kilogram of dinitrophenol, and that determination of the amount of alcohol in the expired air showed only a small part of this increase to be due to elimination by this route. They stress the fact that the dosage employed would be definitely dangerous in man, and therefore that the use of dinitrophenol clinically in acute alcoholic intoxication is not practicable.

The effect of relatively safe doses in man was investigated by Newman and Cutting (43). A test dose of 0.5 cc. of alcohol per kilogram body weight was administered intravenously to a subject, and the rate of fall of the blood alcohol concentration determined at intervals. Subsequently the subject was given 100 mgm. dinitrophenol by mouth three times daily for a period of two weeks, during which time there was an increase of 40% in her basal metabolic rate. In spite of this, on the administration of another test dose of alcohol the rate of fall of the blood alcohol concentration was found to be identical with the first trial. Another subject was given 1.5 cc. of alcohol per kilogram as a 20% solution in normal saline in one hour, the intravenous route being employed. An hour was allowed to elapse for equilibration between the blood and tissues, and then the rate of decline of the blood alcohol followed at hourly intervals for two hours, at the end of which time 500 mgm. of dinitrophenol was administered by mouth and the blood alcohol again was determined at hourly intervals. There was no increase of the rate of alcohol metabolism with this dose, which, although it did not produce a rise in body temperature or respiratory rate, was as high as could be routinely administered to man with any degree of safety.

Newman and Tainter investigated this problem (44) further in the dog. Alcohol was administered in a dose of 4 cc. per kilogram by slow intravenous injection, producing light anesthesia in all cases, under which the trachea was connected by a cannula to a basal-metabolism apparatus provided with a motor blower. When restlessness required further anesthesia, pentobarbital was administered intravenously in divided doses, the maximum amount in any dog being 15 mgm. per kilogram during the course of the experiment. After the alcohol injection, at least one hour was allowed to elapse for equilibration of alcohol between the blood and tissues. Then samples of venous blood were obtained at hourly intervals and analyzed for alcohol. After a two-hour control period, 6 to 10 mgm. of dinitrophenol per kilogram were administered intramuscularly. Then, for two hours, the animal was either made to breathe room air or in and out of the closed system of the metabolism apparatus. The oxygen of the closed system was replenished as needed, and carbon dioxide was absorbed in the usual manner with soda lime. Oil was used in the spirometer rather than water, to avoid absorption of alcohol, which control observations demonstrated it did effectively. After the second two-hour period the procedure was reversed, those animals which had first breathed room air breathing into the machine and vice versa. Respiratory rates and volumes, and oxygen consumption were recorded graphically by the metabolism machine. By this technic the elimination of alcohol in the expired air could be prevented, since when breathing into the metabolism machine the small volume of air so represented soon came into equilibrium with the alveolar alcohol tension and no further alcohol was lost from the body by this route. On an average of five experiments, dinitrophenol increased the oxygen consumption to from 322 to 630% of the control values, with an average increase of body temperature of 2.7° C. At the same time the respiratory volume increased to an average of about 1,200% of the control volumes. In the control periods the blood alcohol fell an average of 21.3 mgm.% per hour. After dinitrophenol, when the respiratory volumes were twelve times the control values, the rate of fall of the blood alcohol remained unchanged as long as the dogs were rebreathing from the metabolism machine and hence not losing alcohol through their breath. But, when they were made to breathe into the room air, the rate of fall of blood alcohol concentration immediately doubled, the average rate of fall being 43.7 mgm.% per hour. Calculation of the amount of alcohol lost in the breath due to this increase in respiratory volume checked closely with the observed increase in rate of elimination of alcohol from the body. Moreover, when the conditions of the experiment were the same, except for elimination of the dinitrophenol and substitution of mechanical hyperventilation by means of a pump producing the same change in respiratory volume, an identical degree of increase in rate of fall of blood alcohol concentration resulted. Thus the evidence is conclusive that the increased elimination of alcohol incidental to the administration of dinitrophenol can be accounted for by increased elimination of alcohol in the expired air, and that the direct stimulant action demonstrated on the liver in vitro must play an insignificant part in the intact animal. It can thus be stated that the two metabolic stimulants, thyroxin and dinitrophenol, are not capable of significantly accelerating the enzymatic action responsible for the initial process of alcohol metabolism.

Fever.—There has been an investigation of the effects of fever on the rate of alcohol metabolism. Fleming and Reynolds (27) gave a dose of 0.6 cc. per kilogram to human subjects intravenously, and found that the blood alcohol curve was lower throughout its extent than was the case with normal temperature. Erwteman and Heeres (16) gave ⅕ gm. per kilogram to men by mouth and found the maximal concentration in the blood to be lower than normal, with a rapid fall thereafter. It is likely that this more rapid metabolism of alcohol indicated by the foregoing work is directly ascribable to the fever, rather than to the accompanying increase in general bodily metabolism, since we have seen that an increase in general metabolism brought about by other means is ineffectual while in the poikilotherm an increase in temperature is effective in increasing the rate of alcohol metabolism. Since in cold-blooded animals the rate of alcohol metabolism has been shown to follow Van't Hoff's coefficient for chemical reactions, if the same situation exists in the homeotherm we would expect a doubling of the rate of alcohol metabolism with an increase in body temperature of 10° C. Such an increase cannot be produced with safety in man, which probably accounts for the not very striking increase in rate reported by the investigators we have quoted.

Oxygen.—Since the metabolism of alcohol to carbon dioxide and water requires the consumption of oxygen, it has occurred to some workers that supplying an excess of this substance might be effective in expediting the process. Fleming and Reynolds (27) found that breathing pure oxygen for 3 hours did not alter the rate of fall of blood alcohol concentration after the intravenous administration of 0.6 cc. per kilogram intravenously in man. Less clearly cut negative results were obtained by McFarland and Barach (45). They tested 23 human subjects after doses of ¾, 1, and 1¼ gm. of alcohol per kilogram by mouth as a 33⅓% solution in water and orange juice, both in air and in 50% oxygen and 2% carbon dioxide. Alcohol was determined at the end of ½, 1, and 2 hours, by a method requiring a sample of 20 cc., which possibly accounts for the few samples taken. In general, blood alcohol concentration was lower at the end of 2 hours when the oxygen–carbon dioxide mixture was breathed; but this was not the case, as noted by the authors, in about 20% of the cases. They were unable to explain the lack of effect in these cases. The obvious criticism of this work is that the observations were made during the period of absorption, when any effect on this function would cloud the issue. Also, it would have been more satisfactory if a mixture of gases had not been given, so that one might be able to place the responsibility for the action, if any, where it rightfully belonged. Thus the experimental evidence does not favor the administration of oxygen in excess of its normal concentration in the air as effective in increasing the rate of alcohol metabolism. This would rather be expected, since with the usual amount of oxygen in the air the oxygen saturation of the blood is practically complete, and the small additional amount that might be carried dissolved in the plasma should not be a very potent factor in the process.

Carbon dioxide.—The effect of 6% carbon dioxide in air on the rate of alcohol combustion was shown by Fleming and Reynolds (27) not to be appreciable when administered for short periods occupying about a third of a total period of four hours after intravenous administration of 0.6 cc. per kilogram intravenously in man. The effect of higher concentrations of carbon dioxide, with or without oxygen, cannot rightfully be considered as due to increased alcohol metabolism, but rather to increased respiratory elimination of alcohol incidental to the hyperpnea produced by the stimulation of respiration by carbon dioxide. This was shown in the dog and in man by Newman and Card (46), and will be discussed in detail when we consider the therapy of acute alcoholism.

Muscular exercise.—A great deal of work has been done on the relation of muscular work to the rate of metabolism of alcohol. Carpenter (47) administered alcohol to hens by keeping them in an atmosphere saturated with alcohol vapor, and determined the alcohol content of their tissues after varying intervals of exposure. He found that hens which were kept hopping about by the administration of induction shocks through the floor of the cage showed in general a lower alcohol concentration of the tissues than hens which were allowed a more sedentary existence. The rather novel method of administration leaves us somewhat in doubt of the meaning of this finding, since exercise surely has an effect on rate and depth of respiration, and since absorption in this case was through the lungs such effects might well overshadow any effect of exercise directly on rate of alcohol metabolism. This interpretation is in accord with later work by the same investigator (48). Doses of 30 and 50 cc. of alcohol were administered to human subjects, and the alcohol content of expired air, urine, and blood followed at intervals. Periods of exercise of one to two hours on a bicycle ergometer at a rate of work of from 275 to 550 kg. m. per minute had no effect on the rate of metabolism of the alcohol, as judged from the rate of disappearance from the body. The amount eliminated in the breath and urine did not change sufficiently to influence the result in any degree.

Canzanelli, Guild, and Rapport (49) determined the effect of exercise on the rate of alcohol metabolism in an 8 kg. bitch, which was made to run on a treadmill for 15 minutes at a speed of 2.5 km. per hour. The criterion of alcohol oxidation was the change in respiratory quotient from the value of 1.0 characteristic of carbohydrate metabolism to the .68 seen when alcohol is burned. By stomach tube, 100 cc. of 10% alcohol was administered, and the R.Q. fell from the pre-alcohol level of .86 to .74. When, however, the animal was required to exercise on the treadmill after being given alcohol, there was no fall of R.Q. apparent. From this the authors conclude that alcohol can be utilized only for vegetative functions. As a matter of fact, their data justify the statement that exercise does not increase the rate of alcohol metabolism but no more.

Probably the best-controlled and most convincing work on this problem was done by Nyman and Palmlov (50). Their subjects were young, healthy men from 21 to 26 years of age. The average dose of alcohol was 0.4 to 0.5 gm. of alcohol per kilogram administered by mouth, and the rate of work investigated 378 kg. m. per minute. Blood alcohol determinations were made on capillary blood by Widmark's method, the blood alcohol concentration being followed over a period of about 4½ hours. In all cases the rate of fall of the blood alcohol was linear, in no way accelerated by periods of exercise. In one case, in which the subject was kept lying down prior to the period of exercise, there was a slight increase in blood alcohol at the onset of work, for which no satisfactory explanation could be found, although it was suggested that possibly it indicated mobilization of alcohol from a hypothetical storage depot. It seems much more reasonable to us that the change in posture was effective in expelling some unabsorbed alcohol from the stomach, with subsequent rapid absorption raising the blood alcohol momentarily.

The foregoing work all depended for the assessment of the rate of alcohol metabolism on changes in respiratory quotient or rate of fall of blood alcohol concentration. LeBreton (51) determined directly the amount of alcohol metabolized with and without muscular exercise in the rat by administration of a known amount of alcohol followed at an interval by analysis of the carcass to determine the amount of alcohol remaining. The amount eliminated in the excreta was also determined, and these two amounts subtracted from the amount administered indicated the amount of alcohol burned during the interval period. Two groups of rats were given 1.5 gm. of alcohol per kilogram intraperitoneally. Then one group was allowed to remain at rest, while the other did sufficient work on a treadmill to increase their metabolic rates from 80 to 180%. There was no significant difference in the rate of alcohol metabolism in the two groups. In another series of rats, the rate of alcohol metabolism at rest was determined on two separate occasions by the indirect method from the blood alcohol curve and subsequently it was determined directly after the animal was forced to exercise. Again the two results checked closely, and the author concluded that alcohol was not utilizable for muscular work. We do not believe the results justify such a conclusion. Certainly it is clear from all of the work reported that exercise is not capable of increasing the rate of metabolism of alcohol, but in no case has it been proved that some of the energy derived from the combustion of alcohol is not used for the production of muscular energy.

It is not surprising that exercise does not affect the rate of alcohol metabolism, when we recollect that this is a function of a specific enzyme system in the liver which works seemingly at full capacity regardless of the amount of alcohol to be metabolized or the need of the body for energy. Thus the liver can be considered as a controlling valve which limits the rate of combustion of alcohol. To give a mechanical analogy, it may be likened to the governor on a stationary engine which maintains the revolutions per minute constant regardless of the amount of gasoline in the tank or the load imposed on the engine.

Availability of energy derived from alcohol.—Once the primary step in alcohol oxidation, which probably consists in the production of acetic acid, has been accomplished in the liver, there is no evidence whatever bearing on the site of the ultimate metabolism to carbon dioxide and water, or even of the possibility of conversion to some substance that might be stored as a source of energy, a concept put forward by Carpenter (52). Thus, to say, as some writers have, that the fact that muscular exercise does not increase the rate of disappearance of alcohol from the body means that none of the energy derived from the combustion of alcohol can be used for muscular work is obviously fallacious.

Following this same type of reasoning, LeBreton (53, 54)

stated the energy of alcohol cannot be used in heat production to combat cold. She gave rats 2 gm. per kilogram of alcohol as a 20% solution subcutaneously, and divided them into two groups, one of which she placed at the neutral temperature of 26° C. and the other at 7° C. for a period of 70 minutes. The metabolic rate of the rats placed at the low environmental temperature increased twofold over that of those at thermal neutrality, without any change in the rate of combustion of alcohol. Thus at thermal neutrality alcohol provided 70% of the metabolic requirement, while at the low temperature it provided but 35%. From this she concluded that alcohol cannot be used in the fight against cold.

It is quite true that a cold environment cannot bring about an increased rate of alcohol metabolism to provide more energy for heat production, but it is not obvious from this that the calories derived from alcohol at its fixed rate of primary metabolism are less useful to the animal in its combat with a cold environment than those derived from fuels which are not subject to such a fixed rate. Nor do we think the concept of LeBreton (53) that metabolic procedures can be divided into three distinct categories, each with its separate enzyme system, subserving muscular contraction, heat production for combating cold, and what she called "elementary cellular metabolism," is on a sound basis or is supported by any factual data. Thus, the fact that alcohol metabolism is limited in its rate by a mechanism which we have dealt with in detail is not evidence sufficient to justify the conclusion that the energy derived from alcohol can be used only for "elementary cellular metabolism"; and it is on this premise that the whole elaborate concept of the physiological significance of alcohol metabolism put forth by LeBreton rests.

Effect of protein.—In recent years, more and more evidence has been amassed linking the metabolism of alcohol with that of other foodstuffs, notably with carbohydrate metabolism. In general, it may be said that the only type of food which is capable, on the administration of a single dose, of changing the rate of alcohol metabolism in the normally nourished animal is protein. We are considering now the effect of food on the metabolism of absorbed alcohol, not on the rate of absorption of alcohol, which as we saw earlier is a function of all food in varying degree. Widmark (55, 20) was the first to note that if amino acids were given with alcohol, there was a lower maximum to the blood alcohol curve, which declined to zero more rapidly than if alcohol were given alone. He evolved a theory to account for this phenomenon which postulates a combination in the alimentary tract of the amino acid and alcohol as an ester that thenceforth does not participate in alcohol metabolism, so that the blood alcohol curve assumes the same form as if a smaller dose of alcohol had been given. This theory would explain the observed facts very nicely; but unfortunately there is no experimental evidence, either in vitro or in vivo, of such a combination. Fortunately, we need not concern ourselves with the search for such evidence; for LeBreton (56) showed the effect to be obtainable on parenteral administration of alcohol. A dose of 1.5 gm. of alcohol per kilogram was administered to rabbits by various routes, and the animals were killed after an interval and the alcohol remaining in the body determined. When either Witte's peptone or *d*-alanine in a dose of 4 gm. per kilogram was administered by mouth three hours before the alcohol administration, there was an increase in the rate of alcohol metabolism of from 40 to 60%, regardless of whether the alcohol was administered by mouth, subcutaneously, intraperitoneally, or intravenously. It is hardly conceivable that after parenteral injection an appreciable quantity of alcohol could be secreted into the gastrointestinal tract, there to combine with the amino acids which should by that time have been completely absorbed, and so deform the blood alcohol curve or the amount of alcohol recoverable from the carcass. Furthermore, Newman (57) demonstrated that even when both the amino acid and the alcohol are administered intravenously the same effect is obtained.

Haggard and Greenberg (24), however, apparently ignorant of the work of LeBreton which had been published some six years previously, repeated the work of Widmark and offered another explanation of his results, which they believed to be due entirely to delay in absorption brought about by the amino acids. This delayed absorption could easily account for the lower maximum concentration of the blood alcohol curve; but it required some elaboration to explain also the more rapid fall to the base line, which it seemed could mean only more rapid combustion of alcohol or the removal of part of the alcohol from the field. The explanation they offered was sufficiently ingenious to deserve to be correct, which we know it was not from the work of LeBreton, which showed conclusively that more rapid metabolism was the factor actually operating. Their explanation does, however, throw some light on the mechanism of metabolism of alcohol, and so warrants consideration in this respect. They found that, if alcohol were administered sufficiently slowly at a constant rate over a long period, combustion kept pace with administration and no considerable concentration in the blood resulted. It was their opinion that the slowing of absorption brought about by amino acids was sufficient when small doses of alcohol were given to permit, during the later hours after administration, combustion of alcohol to outstrip the slow and prolonged absorption, with the result that the blood alcohol concentration fell to zero and remained there in spite of the fact that active combustion of alcohol was still taking place. Possibly this factor does play some part in the effect of amino acids when they and alcohol are administered by mouth, but it must be conceded that the main effect is one on speed of alcohol combustion.

This thesis is supported by the recent work of Eggleton (25), who showed that the effect, which in her cats lasted but an hour and a half when a single dose of amino acid was given, could be prolonged indefinitely by a slow, continuous infusion of the amino acid. This transitory nature of the accelerating action of amino acids she invokes in her explanation of the fact that the rate of fall of the blood alcohol curve when amino acids are given before the administration of alcohol is on a lower level throughout but parallel to that with alcohol alone. With a more rapid metabolic rate over the whole period we would expect the slope of the curve with amino acids to be steeper. Eggleton's explanation why this is not the case is that the full accelerating effect of the amino acid is expended during the absorptive phase, so that during this period more alcohol is burned and the maximum is lower, but that by the time the steady rate of fall of blood alcohol concentration is apparent the effect is no longer operative and thus the rate of fall is the same as with alcohol alone.

That the effect of amino acids is exerted directly on the metabolic process in the liver is supported by the work of Leloir and Munoz (9), who showed that in vitro alanine was effective in slightly increasing the rate of alcohol metabolism. Just what is the mechanism of the acceleration of alcohol combustion by amino acids is not known. The possibility of its being associated in some way with the specific dynamic action of protein suggests itself; but further investigation is needed before we can even speculate intelligently regarding this problem.

Fat.—Fats administered by mouth at the same time alcohol is given by the same route will slow absorption of alcohol, but Fleming and Reynolds (27) demonstrated that the oral administration of 290 cc. of olive oil to a subject prior to the intravenous injection of 0.6 cc. per kilogram of alcohol did not in any way alter the resulting curve of blood alcohol concentration. This and other evidence indicates that single doses of fat, fatty acids, or glycerol have no effect on the metabolic rate of alcohol.

Carbohydrate.—The result of the administration of carbohydrates, particularly glucose, in single doses on the rate of alcohol metabolism is in dispute. Leloir and Munoz (9) found on one occasion that glucose added to the substrate caused a slightly increased rate of metabolism of alcohol by liver in vitro but this was by no means constant and not at all of the magnitude of the changes brought about by agents such as pyruvic acid.

Goldfarb and Bowman (58) found that the addition of 1% glucose greatly accelerated the oxidation of alcohol in vitro with hydrogen peroxide. It need hardly be pointed out that this is rather a far departure from conditions in vivo.

Chapheau (59) administered iodoacetic acid 70 mg. per kilogram to rabbits, resulting in nonutilization of glucose and a rise in blood sugar from 130 mgm.% to 210 to 215 mgm.%, without any change in the rate of disappearance of alcohol after the ingestion of a dose of 2 cc. per kilogram; nor was the depletion of the glycogen store by administration of 250 mgm. per kilogram of phlorizin daily for a week effective in producing a change.

Goldfarb, Bowman, and Parker (30) administered 50 cc. of 50% glucose to a series of acute alcoholics, and compared the rate of fall of blood alcohol concentration with that in controls to whom no glucose was given. They divided the subjects into two groups—the moderately intoxicated with blood alcohol concentrations below 300 mgm.%, and the severely intoxicated with concentrations above this figure. The fall in blood alcohol concentration in the two-hour period after the administration of the glucose was not different from that in a similar period in the controls so far as the moderately intoxicated individuals were concerned; but with the severely intoxicated it was considerably greater—110 mgm.% as against 53 mgm.% for the controls. The failure of glucose to effect an acceleration in all cases is ascribed by the authors to inability of these subjects to utilize glucose. Why glucose seems to work in the severely intoxicated while it is ineffective in the moderately intoxicated is not satisfactorily explained.

On the other hand, Bickel (60) is reported as finding that the blood alcohol curve in rabbits sinks more slowly when alcohol and sugar are given than is the case with alcohol alone.

Our own experience (61) with this subject is not as complete as it might be. It consists essentially of the observation in dogs that the acceleration of alcohol metabolism brought about by insulin, of which more later, was neither increased nor decreased by simultaneous administration of sufficient glucose to cover the insulin dosage, plus repeated doses of glucose by stomach tube during the period of decline of blood alcohol concentration. The effect of glucose alone on alcohol metabolism was not directly investigated in the dog. Additional data bearing on the problem were obtained in 1932 when we made our first intravenous injections of alcohol in man. At the onset, following the technic of those who had used alcohol as an intravenous anesthetic (62), the alcohol was administered in a 33⅓% glucose solution; but later we felt that the elimination of the glucose, which we found to be quite safe, was desirable. Therefore we were able to compare, in the same individual, the blood alcohol curves after a dose of 1.0 cc. per kilogram of alcohol administered intravenously both in a vehicle of 33⅓% glucose and in normal saline. There was not the slightest difference in either the height to which the blood alcohol concentration rose or the steepness of the decline with the two procedures.

Carpenter investigated the effect of several sugars on the rate of alcohol metabolism in man. Unfortunately, he determined the length of time alcohol remained in the body by the time necessary for it to disappear from the breath. That this expedient was not entirely satisfactory can be deduced from the author's comments. The simultaneous measurement of the gaseous metabolism precluded the taking of repeated blood samples, so the breath determinations had to be substituted. Also unfortunate was the administration of both the alcohol and the sugars by mouth, with the possibility of an influence on absorption being mistaken for one on metabolism. That the latter is not a remote possibility is supported by the finding by the author that alcohol definitely increased the speed of absorption of galactose, so that a reciprocal activity of galactose on alcohol absorption cannot be summarily denied. In the investigation of the effect of glucose, Carpenter (2) gave doses of 10, 15, and 20 cc. of alcohol as a 5% solution with 31, 46.5, and 62 gm. of glucose by mouth, the glucose dosage being isomolecular with the alcohol. With the 15 cc. dose of alcohol, alcohol disappeared from the expired air in, on an average, 138 minutes in controls and 115 minutes when glucose was given as well. This evidence was considered as indicative of more rapid oxidation of alcohol brought about by the glucose. That it could equally well be due to slowing of absorption was not considered. The gaseous exchange studies showed that the combustion of alcohol caused an increase of but 3.5% in basal metabolic rate, which is only a very small fraction of the caloric value of the alcohol. Glucose was found to cause about half as great an increase, and the two agents together effected an increment equal to the simple sum of each given separately. Thus the evidence points to the increase in metabolism of alcohol brought about by glucose, if such in fact exists, being utilized in the normal bodily metabolism just as is the case when no sugar is given. Of this we shall have more to say shortly.

When galactose (63) was substituted for glucose in the same dosage, alcohol was present in the expired air for 155 minutes as against 138 minutes for the controls without galactose, indicating that galactose slows the metabolism of alcohol. Again the factor of absorption is not considered, in spite of the fact that the increased galactosuria with alcohol is ascribed to more rapid absorption of galactose brought about by alcohol.

The action of fructose (52) is qualitatively like that of glucose, but greater in degree, alcohol disappearing from the expired air in 105 minutes compared with 138 in the controls. The authors noted that if it is assumed that all the alcohol ingested was metabolized in the period by the end of which alcohol had disappeared from the breath, the percentage of the total metabolic requirement that would be so represented would be so great as to indicate an impossibility. They suggested, therefore, that the alcohol was not entirely metabolized but rather might have been transformed to some other substance. Is it not equally possible that the whole effect was one of delayed and slowed absorption, which could, as explained by Haggard and Greenberg (24), cause the blood alcohol concentration, and consequently the alcohol content of the expired air, to fall to the base line while active alcohol metabolism was still going on? Until it has been more conclusively shown that, apart from any possibility of an effect on absorption, fructose or glucose actually speeds up the metabolism of alcohol, it is hardly worth while entering the field of speculation as to how the body is able to use up the energy produced.

Clark and Morrissey (64) gave a dose of alcohol of 3 gm. per kilogram to dogs and determined their blood alcohol concentrations at hourly intervals for 6 to 8 hours to establish control curves. Then the animals were given the same dose, blood alcohol was determined hourly for 3 to 4 hours as a control period, and then glucose was given and the blood alcohol followed 3 to 5 hours longer. In no case did glucose change the rate of disappearance of alcohol from the blood.

We can thus say that there is no clear-cut, well-controlled experimental evidence which unequivocally shows glucose to be effective in accelerating the rate of alcohol metabolism when given in a single dose to an animal in a normal state of nutrition. A repetition of some of the work with certain factors such as absorption better controlled is indicated to clarify the issue.

Insulin.—Supniewski (65) first investigated the effect of insulin on the rate of metabolism of alcohol. He gave 2 rabbits .25 gm. per kilogram of alcohol subcutaneously, and at the end of 45 minutes found the blood alcohol concentrations to be 16.4 and 9.8 mg.%. The next day the procedure was repeated, except that one unit of insulin was given with the alcohol, and the blood alcohol concentrations at 45 minutes were 11.1 and 5.2 mg.%, indicating an increased rate of metabolism. This increased rate of metabolism was borne out by studies on acetaldehyde formation. Alcohol administration was shown to increase the acetaldehyde content of the blood of rabbits, indicating that it might be an intermediary product in alcohol metabolism. The administration of 2.5 cc. per kilogram of alcohol raised the blood acetaldehyde to 1.5 mg.%. When insulin was given with the alcohol, however, this increased markedly to 3.4 mg.%. This would indicate that insulin accelerates the initial process of oxidation of alcohol, with the result that there is an accumulation of intermediary products in the blood stream.

Several investigators have been unable to confirm the accelerating action of insulin on alcohol metabolism. Thus Fleming and Reynolds (27) found that in man, after the intravenous administration of 0.6 cc. per kilogram of alcohol intravenously, the administration of 10 units of insulin produced no change in the slope of the blood alcohol curve. This work can be criticized on the standpoint of inadequate dosage, as those investigators who have demonstrated an effect employed larger doses. The same criticism cannot be applied to the work of Harger and Hulpieu (41), who employed a dose of insulin of 1 unit per kilogram either with or without enough glucose to prevent a drop in blood sugar, and found this to be ineffective in influencing the blood alcohol curve in dogs given 1.5 to 3.0 gm. per kilogram of alcohol by stomach tube.

Hirschfelder and Maxwell (66) thought that they had evidence pointing to a lack of effect of insulin on alcohol metabolism. They gave 2.0 to 4.0 cc. per kilogram of alcohol to rabbits, with and without 1½ to 3 units per kilogram of insulin, and found the insulin not to be capable of ameliorating the toxic symptoms of the alcohol. No effort was made to trace the disappearance of the alcohol from the body. When it is considered that such doses of insulin are themselves capable of producing symptoms quite like those of acute alcoholism, it will be readily seen that the evidence presented lacks any real bearing on the point at issue. They noted the interesting fact that administration of alcohol did not check insulin convulsions, indicating that the lack of glucose for cerebral oxidative processes cannot be made up for by alcohol, a finding which has recently been confirmed by Goldfarb and Wortis (67).

In spite of this negative evidence, the majority of investigators have confirmed Supniewski's finding. Widmark (40) administered alcohol to dogs by mouth in a dose of 2 cc. per kilogram, and found that .85 unit of insulin per kilogram was effective in bringing about an increase in rate of disappearance of up to 100%. This increase was greatest in those dogs which burned alcohol slowly, and varied from day to day in the same animal. Serianni (68) found that in man the injection of 20 units of insulin 40 to 113 minutes before giving alcohol by mouth was effective in accelerating the fall of blood alcohol concentration from 41 to 50%. In patients with cirrhosis of the liver no such acceleration took place, from which he concluded that an action on the normal liver must be involved. Bickel (60) was reported as saying that insulin accelerated the metabolism of alcohol but that if sugar were given with the insulin this acceleration did not take place.

Newman and Cutting (43) gave two human subjects a test dose of 1.5 cc. of alcohol by vein, and after an interval of an hour for equilibration blood alcohol determinations were run hourly for three hours, at which time 1 unit of insulin per kilogram was administered hypodermically, the simultaneous administration of 200 gm. of glucose in a small amount of water being effected by mouth. Hourly blood samples were taken subsequent to the injection until the blood alcohol concentration reached the base line. At no time were there evidences of hypoglycemia. The increase in rate of alcohol metabolism amounted to 40% in one of the subjects and to 54% in the other. Similar results were obtained in the same subjects by the administration of so-called insulin-free pancreatic extract, and the authors mentioned the possibility of the action being due to some other component of pancreatic extracts than insulin. Subsequent investigation has shown, however, that the supposedly insulin-free extract did in fact contain appreciable amounts of insulin, as indicated by its ability to markedly reduce blood sugar (69). Clark and Morrissey (64) found that 1 to 2 units of insulin per kilogram in the dog were effective in increasing the rate of metabolism of a dose of 3 gm. of alcohol per kilogram, as indicated by an increase of rate of fall of blood alcohol concentration of 20 to 50 mg. in 2 to 4 hours. When glucose and an alkalizing salt, such as sodium bicarbonate or citrate, which in themselves were not effective in accelerating alcohol metabolism, were administered with the insulin its effect was enhanced. These investigators believed that acceleration of glucose oxidation by insulin catalyzed alcohol metabolism. They were unable to increase the rate of disappearance of alcohol brought about by liver in vitro by addition of insulin. Newman and Cutting (43) believed that they had accomplished this; but the fact that the increases they reported were very small, and that they obtained similar increases when liver was omitted from the system, makes their evidence inconclusive. There has to our knowledge been no attempt to demonstrate the insulin effect in the perfused liver, an effect which has been shown to occur in the metabolism of propylene glycol by the perfused cat liver (13). Incidentally, it has been shown (70) that if urinary excretion is eliminated by nephrectomy the rate of metabolism of this dihydroxy alcohol is constant, and that its metabolism proceeds in the isolated perfused cat liver at a constant rate. Thus it is of interest to note that the resemblance to alcohol metabolism is still further carried out in its acceleration by insulin, which should be confirmed in the intact animal.

Alcohol metabolism in diabetes.—Clark, Morrissey, and Fazekas (71) performed experiments with the liver of diabetic cats in vitro that indicated an important role of insulin in alcohol metabolism. They aseptically removed the pancreas from cats, and when diabetes was maximally established killed the animals and immediately removed the liver. There were 500 mg. of liver slices placed in 125 cc. glass-stoppered, Erlenmeyer flasks, suspended in 6 cc. of phosphate buffer pH 7.4 containing 2.5 mg. of alcohol, and agitated at 37° C. for three hours. Controls were run with liver tissue killed by heat. At the end of the incubation period the contents of the flasks were precipitated with zinc sulphate and steam distilled, alcohol being determined by the method of Harger. In 19 observations on the livers of 8 normal cats 23.5% of the alcohol disappeared in the three-hour period, the range being from 16 to 39%. In 17 observations on the livers of 7 cats depancreatized 72 to 96 hours before death the average disappearance was 3.1%, with a range of 0.5 to 6.2%, while in one depancreatized cat maintained on insulin it was 36%. With 2 cats, pancreatectomy was performed and diabetes allowed to develop, at which time a sample of liver was removed at biopsy and tested for alcohol metabolism. Then 10 to 14 units of insulin were given the cats, and after 5 hours they were killed and a second sample of liver obtained. The amounts of alcohol metabolized by the first samples were 0.3 and 0.56%; and those by the second, obtained after insulin, were 29.4 and 27.5%. This evidence is certainly strongly in favor of insulin being necessary for alcohol metabolism by the liver of the cat. Unfortunately, the workers did not add insulin to the flasks directly; so we cannot be sure that the insulin effect was not due to some change in the liver produced by the insulin in vivo.

Mirsky and Nelson (17) investigated the effect of pancreatectomy on alcohol metabolism in vivo. They administered 1 cc. of alcohol per kilogram as a 20% solution intravenously to unanesthetized dogs, and found the rate of decline of the blood alcohol curve to be constant. This rate was slightly decreased by a fast of 96 hours, being immediately returned to normal by the administration of food. The dogs were then depancreatized, and the test dose was given at 64 and 88 hours later, at which time the curves were identical with those in the normal state. At 96 hours there was a slight slowing of the rate, but not more than that demonstrated in normal dogs after such a period of fasting. Administration of insulin and glucose to the depancreatized dogs in no way changed the rate of alcohol metabolism. This certainly indicates that in the dog alcohol metabolism may proceed at a normal rate without the presence of the pancreas, and is in direct controversy with the findings in vitro of Clark, Morrissey, and Fazekas. In spite of the very different experimental situation existing in the two experiments, it is very difficult to reconcile the divergent results obtained; and further work is certainly indicated before we are justified in forming any definite conclusions regarding the actual role of insulin in alcohol metabolism.

When we look for help in this problem to work done with diabetic human subjects, we again find the results to be controversial. Erwteman and Heeres (16) gave ⅕ gm. of alcohol per kilogram by mouth to normal subjects and to diabetics, and found that in diabetes the maximum concentration attained was higher and the rate of fall slower. When the diabetics were maintained on an adequate carbohydrate intake, however, the curve became normal, and the authors attribute the abnormal curves to lack of liver glycogen when carbohydrate intake was not adequate. Mirsky and Nelson criticize this work on the valid basis that the administration of alcohol by mouth entails the variable factor of absorption.

Blotner (72) administered 0.6 cc. per kilogram of alcohol by mouth as a 20% solution in grape juice and water to a group of normal fasting subjects, and so determined a normal alcohol-tolerance curve by analysis of the blood and urine at half-hourly intervals for four hours after ingestion. In 6 patients with diabetes mellitus the maximum concentration was higher, but the rate of fall was as fast or faster than that of the normal controls. Again the factor of absorption enters into our appraisal of these results; but they certainly do not support the thesis that insulin is necessary for normal alcohol metabolism.

Synergism of glucose and insulin.—Some workers have found a considerable synergism between glucose and insulin in the acceleration of alcohol metabolism, although Bickel (60) reported that simultaneous administration of glucose prevented the acceleration by insulin, and Harger and Hulpieu (41) found no effect from the combination of the two agents. Clark and Morrissey (64) reported that the addition of glucose and an alkalizing salt slightly enhanced the activity of insulin on alcohol metabolism.

Goldfarb, Bowman, and Parker (30) and Wortis, Bowman, and Goldfarb (73) found a truly astonishing acceleration of the disappearance of alcohol from the blood of acute alcoholics treated with insulin and glucose. In the first study, a group of acute alcoholics, divided roughly into those whose blood alcohol concentration at the institution of treatment was above 300 mg.% (who were termed severely intoxicated) and those with lower blood alcohol values (who were termed moderately intoxicated), were separated into four categories according to the treatment they received. In all cases the initial blood alcohol determination was followed by another at the end of two hours, so that the rate of fall of the blood alcohol concentration during this period was known. The control group received no active treatment, and the average rate of fall of blood alcohol was 53 mg.% in the severely and 48 mg.% in the moderately intoxicated. The next group received 15 units of insulin subcutaneously when the first blood sample was taken, and here the rate of fall was 53 mg.% in both severely and moderately intoxicated—so close to the control values as to indicate no effect of this dosage of insulin alone. The third group received an intravenous injection of 50 cc. of 50% glucose, with a rate of fall of 49 mg.% in the moderately intoxicated and 110 mg.% in the severely intoxicated. Thus glucose alone seemed effective, but only with high blood alcohol concentrations. To the fourth group both insulin and glucose were given, with very striking results. The rate of fall in the moderately intoxicated was 86 mg.% and in the severely intoxicated 167 mg.%, indicating a very definite synergism. The workers believed that the reason glucose alone did not always effect an acceleration was that in some subjects it was not utilized because of some hypothetical effect of alcoholic excess. Since those individuals in which it did not work were those with the lowest blood alcohol values, this explanation seems a little weak. The second paper reported a case of an acute alcoholic whose blood alcohol was lowered from 325 mg.% to 25 mg.% in 4 hours when 15 units of insulin and 25 gm. of glucose were given, a drop which in another patient without benefit of this therapy required 12 hours.

The rather astonishing increase in the rate of alcohol metabolism brought about by glucose and insulin in quite moderate dosage in these patients would seem to be of definite therapeutic value, if confirmed by other observers. The observations are also extremely interesting from the biochemical standpoint, as they are somewhat at variance with our concepts of alcohol metabolism. The investigators reported one case in which the blood alcohol fell 275 mg.% in a period of 2 hours. This is indicative of the elimination of something over 130 gm. of alcohol during this period, assuming the subject to have been a man of 70 kg. If we further assume that the combustion of the alcohol proceeding to completion, 910 calories would have been produced. Now the resting metabolic rate of such a man would not normally exceed 160 calories over a two-hour period; and since all previous work has indicated that alcohol has no appreciable effect on basal metabolic rate, it is difficult to conceive what became of this energy. We know, furthermore, that there is no possibility of excretion of such a quantity of alcohol in that period. The only alternative open is that the alcohol was not burned but was transformed to some other substance, which may or may not have been stored in some particular tissue. We have no proof either for or against this possibility, which we have mentioned before. When, however, we recall that a fall in blood alcohol concentration of 275 mg.% indicates a metabolic rate of alcohol some ten times that seen in normal man, it is hard to understand why some of the previous investigators failed to notice such gross changes in their investigations of the action of glucose and insulin in both man and animals. Thus Newman and Cutting (43) gave much larger doses of insulin and glucose to men, yet the increase in rate they obtained was not over 50%. The objection may be raised that they gave the glucose by mouth rather than intravenously, but their work with the same agents in dogs when glucose was given intravenously yielded no greater acceleration than in man. It therefore seems clear that the results require careful confirmation, preferably in a situation where extraneous factors are better subject to control.

There are but two alternatives in the explanation of the apparent tremendous increase in alcohol metabolism brought about by glucose and insulin; either the alcohol is not burned completely, but is transformed into some other substance that may be either stored indefinitely in the body or metabolized further at a slow rate; or the observations themselves are for some reason unreliable. Should the first alternative be correct, a nice biochemical problem is raised as to what the process of transformation is and what the product formed may be, which may well answer whether or not it may be stored for future use. If such a transformation can take place after insulin and glucose therapy, there is every reason to believe that it may be a normal mode of alcohol metabolism, since these two agents are constantly available in the body. Should this prove to be the case, the role of alcohol as a food would be considerably altered from the present conception of its ability to replace isodynamic quantities of other foodstuffs but not to be available for muscular work or to combat cold or to be stored in the body for future use.

Intriguing as this possible explanation may be, the fact that administration of comparable doses of insulin and glucose to experimental animals and men under conditions much more readily controlled than those existing in a receiving ward for alcoholics has not been productive of comparable results makes it rather unlikely. It is to be hoped that further data may soon be available on this point.

So far we have been considering only the effect of single doses of the various foodstuffs on the rate of alcohol metabolism in animals in a normal state of nutrition. Under these conditions the preponderance of evidence indicates a lack of any action of fat and carbohydrate, with a transitory acceleration of rate with protein administration. Now we shall examine the evidence regarding the effects of fasting and of foodstuffs administered in large amounts over extended periods.

Effect of fasting.—We have already noted that Mirsky and Nelson (17) found that a fast of 96 hours somewhat reduced the rate of alcohol metabolism in the unanesthetized dog. Leloir and Munoz (9) showed that liver obtained from fasted rats metabolized alcohol in vitro at a slower rate than did normal rat liver. LeBreton (74) investigated the problem in the intact white rat. Male rats of the same age were used, kept at 26° C., with water available at all times. The control rats were maintained on a carbohydrate regime, and to insure their having adequate sugar 2 cc. of 40% glucose was given by stomach tube 2 hours before the intraperitoneal injection of 1.5 gm. per kilogram of alcohol. Ninety minutes later the rats were killed, and the amount remaining in their carcasses was analyzed. From this the rate of alcohol metabolism was calculated in milligrams per kilogram per hour. An entirely similar procedure was carried out with rats fasted for different periods which had not, of course, been given the glucose. After a fast of 36 hours the rate had decreased 19%, after one of 48 hours 44%, and after one of 6 days 48%. During the same period the basal metabolic rate decreased only 14 to 30%; so LeBreton concluded that the disproportionate lowering of alcohol metabolism must have been due to an effect of fasting on a specific enzyme system. It occurs to us that a correlation between the lowering of alcohol metabolism and the lowering of liver weight brought about by fasting might be interesting, and quite possibly would adequately explain the changes. Addis, Poo, and Lew (75) demonstrated that a fast of 7 days in the rat reduced the liver protein by 40%, an amount disproportionately large compared with loss of body weight in general, while a fast of but 48 hours reduced it (76) by 20%. These reductions, possibly only coincidentally, are just of the right order of magnitude to account for the reduction of rate of alcohol metabolism. The fact that restoration of food brings a very prompt return to a normal rate is consonant with the finding by these same workers (77) that a very considerable proportion of the lost liver protein may be restored within a day.

Dontcheff (78), using the same method as LeBreton, prolonged the period of fasting to 12 days, during which time the weight of the rats decreased 37% and their rate of oxygen consumption 10 to 15%. The rate of alcohol metabolism dropped 40% between the fourth and sixth days, but then increased, so that from the ninth to the twelfth day it was only 20% lower than normal. This second rise is attributed to the exhausting of the fat reserves, with the coincident starting of metabolism of body proteins. Addis (76) has, however, demonstrated conclusively that body proteins are actively metabolized as early as two days after starting to fast; so this explanation seems untenable. Addis felt that the early loss of protein from the liver indicated that this organ acted as a storehouse for protein in case of need. It is quite possible that when this reserve is exhausted the liver no longer suffers loss of substance, with the result that as the body weight further diminishes the liver comes to represent a greater proportion of total weight, with a resultant increase in rate of alcohol metabolism per unit body weight as found by Dontcheff. Further investigations of the loss of liver protein after longer periods of fasting are needed to support this hypothesis.

A fact not at all in accord with the theory we have advanced is the finding by Dontcheff (79) that after a fast of from 48 hours to 5 days the administration of a single dose of carbohydrate restored the rate of alcohol metabolism to normal. After 10 days of fasting the rate returns not only to normal but above. Protein administration accomplishes essentially the same result, while fats on the other hand have no effect. As a matter of fact, he demonstrated that the administration of a high fat meal after rats had been maintained on a fat diet for only 24 to 48 hours effectively lowered the rate of alcohol metabolism. Thus it would seem that although glucose has no effect on the rate of alcohol metabolism when the animal is in a normal state of nutrition, the maintenance of a normal rate of alcohol metabolism is contingent on the simultaneous combustion of glucose, and when this is interfered with either by starvation or the feeding of an exclusively fat diet the rate falls. What the nature of this interdependence between alcohol and carbohydrate metabolism may be remains obscure. It is possible that the oxidation of the intermediary products of alcohol metabolism may be coupled in some way with the oxidation of glucose, and that when glucose is not being burned the accumulation of these products, by the law of mass action, slows the primary metabolism of alcohol by the liver. Since we have no direct knowledge of the nature of these intermediary products, there is no evidence to support or refute this theory. It is to be hoped that a thorough biochemical investigation of this phase of alcohol metabolism may be forthcoming; for it is of fundamental importance.

Habituation.—A great deal of work has been done in an attempt to explain the well-recognized clinical observation that certain individuals accustomed to the use of alcohol are able to consume larger quantities of alcoholic beverages without evidence of drunkenness than the average occasional drinker. It is at once apparent that this may be due to a number of factors, if we are willing to grant that it actually exists. This whole problem we shall consider in a later chapter, and shall concern ourselves here only with the effect of habitual imbibition of alcohol on the rate of alcohol metabolism.

The statement has been made, apparently on purely hypothetical grounds, that (80) while the normal man oxidizes alcohol only or mainly in the liver, the habituated individual oxidizes it also in the heart, lungs, and muscles. The source of this information is not revealed; but, purely speculative as it may have been, it has received some experimental support. Thus Leloir and Munoz (9) found that rat kidney was capable of causing some slight disappearance of alcohol from the Warburg flask in vitro, and that this was more pronounced in an experiment in which the kidney was obtained from rats habituated to alcohol in a dose of 10 cc. per kilogram per day for one month. The amount of alcohol disposed of was, however, insignificant in comparison with that metabolized by an equal amount of liver.

There are few satisfactory data on the effect of habituation on the rate of alcohol metabolism in man, and these consist almost exclusively of a comparison of the rate of alcohol metabolism as judged from the blood alcohol curve in groups of habituated and nonhabituated individuals which may differ from each other in many respects other than in their consumption of alcohol. Fleming and Stotz (81) administered a dose of 0.6 cc. per kilogram orally to groups of subjects comprising abstainers, moderate drinkers, and heavy drinkers. They found that the blood alcohol concentration of the heavy drinkers rose more rapidly to a higher maximum and fell more rapidly than in the abstainers, the moderate drinkers occupying an intermediate position. Subsequently (28) they varied the procedure by the administration of the alcohol intravenously rather than orally, and found that the differences shown by the preceding series had disappeared, the blood alcohol curves of the three groups being practically identical. Their conclusion, which is the only tenable one, was that the differences with oral administration were due to unequal rates of absorption in the three groups, the habituated individuals absorbing alcohol more promptly than the abstainers, a finding which, as we noted in a preceding chapter, was later confirmed in dogs.

Since it is hardly practicable to render human subjects experimentally habituated to alcohol it has been necessary to employ animal experimentation for carefully controlled work entailing comparison of various factors before and after habituation. Since it has been repeatedly demonstrated that the metabolism of alcohol in such species as the dog, the cat, and the rat does not differ in any essential from that in man, there is no valid objection to application of findings in these animals to man.

Levy (82) habituated rats to alcohol by administration of increasing daily doses by stomach tube, the ultimate dosage attained being over 5 gm. per kilogram and the period of habituation up to 152 days. After the period of habituation the rats were given a dose of 2.16 gm. per kilogram intravenously by rapid injection and were sacrificed at varying intervals, the alcohol content of the blood, brain, kidneys, and liver being determined. Similar determinations on a group of normal controls yielded identical results, indicating that the period of habituation had not been effective in increasing the rate of alcohol metabolism.

Newman and Lehman (83) performed an essentially similar experiment. They habituated a group of 28 rats to alcohol by allowing them as their sole source of fluid a solution of 10% alcohol for a period of 163 days. During this time, they consumed approximately 12 cc. of alcohol per kilogram per day. A control group was treated identically, except for the omission of the alcohol from their drinking water. At the end of the period of habituation all rats were given a dose of 4.0 cc. per kilogram intravenously, the injection requiring less than five minutes. Subgroups of each series were sacrificed at 1, 2, 4, and 6 hours after injection. The curves of blood alcohol concentration so obtained were not significantly different in the two groups, confirming the finding of Levy.

Newman and Cutting (84, 85) reported similar results in dogs, and their work is the more valid because the habituated animals were compared with their own controls before habituation. Three dogs were used, each being given a test dose of 100 cc. of 20% alcohol intravenously to delineate the control curve of blood alcohol. They were then given 5% alcohol as their sole source of fluid for a period of 43 days, at the end of which time they were again given the test dose of 100 cc. of 20% alcohol, having consumed on an average 5.57 cc. of alcohol per kilogram per day during the period of habituation. There was no significant change in the blood alcohol curves of the three dogs after this period, nor after a subsequent period of 47 days on 7.5% alcohol and a still longer period of 10 months on 10%

alcohol during which the daily intake rose to 6.8 cc. per kilogram. It will be noted that doubling the concentration of alcohol in the drinking water increased the alcohol consumption by only about 20%; and it was found that further increase in concentration resulted in death of animals from dehydration, the animals being unable to secure sufficient fluid without coincidentally ingesting a fatal dose of alcohol. Thus we feel that the amount of alcohol ingested was about the maximal compatible with life. As a matter of fact it represents about 60% more than the theoretical maximum that can be oxidized by the dog as determined by Mellanby (19).

Since when the dogs were allowed access to the alcohol solution all during the day they never drank much at any one time, and consequently never became obviously drunk, it was felt that this might be an objection to the validity of the conclusion that habituation did not affect the rate of metabolism. Therefore Newman and Lehman (83) habituated another series of dogs, 5 in number, after having determined their control or abstinent blood alcohol curves after intravenous injection of a test dose of 4.0 cc. per kilogram. These animals were allowed to drink as much as they desired of a 10% alcohol solution during two periods of an hour, one in the morning and the other in the evening. No fluid was permitted during the remainder of the day. They were thus forced, without resorting to tube feeding, to take large quantities of alcohol twice daily, consuming 6.9 cc. per kilogram per day, approximately the same as did the first group of dogs when allowed continuous access to the solution. This resulted in definite evidences of intoxication; and, although the animals maintained their body weight, they showed evidence of poor condition of the coat and a deterioration of disposition not manifest in the first series. The period of habituation was 97 days, at the end of which time the test dose was again administered. It was found that the rate of decline of blood alcohol concentration was 10% more rapid than before habituation, a figure well within the range of variation and of error of the method.

Eggleton (25) has determined the effect of habituation on the rate of alcohol metabolism in cats. She attempted the habituation of 16 cats by giving them as their sole food source milk containing 5% alcohol by weight, left with them overnight. No mention of other sources of fluid was made. Nine of the animals refused the milk, and after a few days were abandoned for the purpose of the experiment. Of these, 3 later showed jaundice or obvious liver disease. The amount of alcohol consumed by the others varied, the largest amount being 3.5 gm. per kilogram per day. The period of habituation varied also, from 13 to 52 days. Of the 7 animals habituated, 2 maintained their body weight, while the remainder lost from 5 to 28%. Of these, 3 showed jaundice, of which 2 had been light drinkers, with an average daily consumption of 0.5 gm. per kilogram per day. From this latter figure, it would seem obvious that a supply of fluid other than the milk must have been available. In this case, the results of habituation to alcohol must have been complicated by those of starvation, a serious criticism when we recall that starvation is known to have a definite effect on alcohol metabolism. The high percentage of cats showing jaundice is remarkable. It seems unlikely that it was due to the alcohol, as it appeared as frequently in those cats which refused to drink. Rather, the cause might be sought in the unhygienic conditions in which London cats have their abode.

The liver weight of the habituated cats was definitely greater in proportion to their body weight than that of their controls—3.4% as against 2.3%. This is in accord with the observed deposition of fat in the livers of animals habituated to alcohol. That other conditions than alcohol consumption have a bearing on liver weight was indicated by the finding that when Eggleton transferred her endeavors from London to Cardiff she found the weight of the livers of Welsh cats to be 3.4% of their body weight, identical with that of the alcoholic London cats. The implication regarding the temperance of Welsh cats is probably not deserved.

After habituation the rate of alcohol metabolism as indicated by the rate of fall of blood alcohol concentration after administration of an intravenous test dose was determined, and it was found that, weight for weight, the alcoholic cats metabolized the same amount of alcohol as their nonalcoholic controls. When the rate of metabolism was related to liver weight, however, the values for the habituated animals were only 50 to 80% of those of the abstinent. The significance of this finding is, we believe, very doubtful as indicating any fundamental change in rate of alcohol metabolism brought about by alcohol habituation. It merely indicates that the addition to liver weight in the habituated cats did not carry with it an increase in the power of the liver as a functional unit in metabolizing alcohol, which is what we should expect, since such increase in weight has been demonstrated to be due to deposition of fat and not to any increase in functional liver parenchyma. That the Welsh cats were really not guilty of tippling on the sly was shown by the fact that they metabolized alcohol at a higher rate than the habituated cats, although the livers of the two groups represented the same percentage of their body weights.

Against this array of evidence, all indicating that habituated animals do not metabolize alcohol any faster than do abstainers, is the work of Gettler and Freireich (86). They used dogs as experimental animals, employing 11 controls and 11 subjected to habituation. The latter were started on 2% alcohol, and gradually worked up to 30%, it being stated that finally each dog consumed about a liter daily of this concentration. Since from their protocols it appears that the average weight of the dogs did not exceed 25 kg., they must have consumed over 12 cc. per kilogram daily, almost twice what Newman and Lehman were successful in administering to their dogs (83), or approximately three times the theoretical maximum daily consumption based on Mellanby's (19) work. Just how this phenomenal consumption of alcohol was accomplished is not clear to us.

The dogs were maintained on this regimen for from 6

months to 2 years. At the end of the period of habituation they were given a test dose of alcohol orally, and were sacrificed at the end of a variable period of time, when the alcohol remaining in their tissues and gastrointestinal tracts was determined. The method of presentation of the data seems unfortunate, in that pairs of experimental animals and controls were compared; and, although the authors stated that they endeavored to match them as closely as possible as to weight, examination of the protocols on the four pairs which are presented in the text show that not only did their weights vary by as much as 20% but that the doses administered and the intervals before death also were not the same for each pair. Because this is the only piece of work controverting the thesis that habituation has no effect on the rate of alcohol metabolism, it is worth while to consider the data in each of the four pairs of dogs presented.

In pair 1, the weight of the animals was about equal—10.0 kg. for the control and 10.7 kg. for the habituated dog. Four grams of alcohol per kilogram were given as a 30% solution by stomach tube, and three-fourths of an hour later the animals were sacrificed. The alcohol concentration in the blood, spinal fluid, brain, and liver of the abstainer was about 75% higher than in the habituated dog. No analysis of the contents of the gastrointestinal tract was made in this case, so that the difference might have been one solely of absorption. In pair 2, the weight of the habituated animal was 18.3 kg. and that of the abstainer 14.7 kg. The former was given about 5 gm. per kilogram, the latter about 3 gm. per kilogram, and the interval before sacrifice was 146 minutes. The tissue alcohol values in the habituated dog were slightly higher; but with the discrepancy in weight and dose, no direct comparison is possible. In pair 3 the habituated animal weighed 23.7 kg. and the control 19.1 kg., and each got a total dose of 45 gm. of alcohol. They were killed at the end of one hour; and the amount of alcohol remaining in the gastrointestinal tract was approximately the same in the two. The tissue alcohol concentrations were about 25% higher in the abstainer; but since the dose for the two was the same and the weight of the abstainer was 20% less, the difference becomes practically nonexistent. In pair 4 the habituated animal weighed 25.9 kg. and the abstainer 20.5 kg. Each received 114 gm. of alcohol, and the abstainer was killed at 53 minutes and the habituated dog at 62 minutes. The amount of unabsorbed alcohol was slightly greater in the abstainer, while the tissue alcohol concentration was almost twice as high in the abstainer as in the habituated dog. These last figures look the most convincing of the lot. However, a little analysis shows this to be more apparent than real. Using Widmark's (20) formula for calculation of the theoretical initial concentration (c_o) of alcohol in the blood, assuming absorption to be immediate and complete, this would have been 530 mgm.% for the habituated dog and 640 mgm.% for the abstainer. The final concentration in the blood for the habituated dog was 248 mgm.%, or a fall of 273 mgm.% per hour; while this same value for the abstainer works out at 253 mgm.% per hour—certainly not a striking difference. However, when we consider that either of these values is about ten times as high as the rate of alcohol metabolism calculated by Mellanby (19), Widmark (20), and other investigators, the validity of the whole experiment becomes open to question.

Therefore, all recent experimentation, with the single exception of that of Gettler and Freireich, has indicated that the consumption of large quantities of alcohol over long periods is not effective in changing the rate at which the organism metabolizes alcohol; and the explanation of tolerance to alcohol must be sought in another direction.

Effect of barbiturates.—The effects of a number of drugs on alcohol metabolism have been investigated. So far as the experimental approach to alcohol metabolism is concerned, the action of anesthetics is of importance, for much of the investigative work has been done on anesthetized animals. We have already seen that chloroform (15, 17) reduces the rate of alcohol metabolism. No data are available on the effects of ether; as a matter of fact, it is probable that the presence of ether would confuse the issue so far as most methods of alcohol analysis are concerned. So far as the barbiturates are concerned, our own impression, based on no particular well-controlled investigation, was that so long as the body temperature and blood pressure were maintained within physiological limits no change in rate of alcohol metabolism occurred. This opinion is concurred in by Eggleton (25), again without direct data. She compared the rate of metabolism of alcohol in milligrams per kilogram per hour in her two series of cats—the London cats with the small livers and the Cardiff cats with the large ones—with Mellanby's and Widmark's dogs, which were not anesthetized, and with her own dogs, which also presumably were not anesthetized. The figures presented by Haggard and Greenberg for dogs were so far out of line as not to be comparable. Her conclusion was that the effect of nembutal, which was the barbiturate she used, was minimal, since the difference in rate between her two groups of cats exceeded the difference between the cats and the dogs of the other investigators. This is not quite a fair assumption, however, since Newman and Lehman (37) have shown that the rate of metabolism in the cat is about 25% higher than that in the dog. However, even on this basis the Cardiff cats measure up to standard, and it is possible that the London cats had other troubles than nembutal to account for their low rate of metabolism. It would therefore seem that the use of a barbiturate as an anesthetic in the investigation of alcohol metabolism need not invalidate the results obtained.

Caffeine.—Koopmann and Kempski (87) found that the drinking of coffee had no effect on the blood alcohol curve, while Fleming and Reynolds (27) demonstrated that the administration of 0.5 gm. of caffeine with a dose of 0.6 cc. of alcohol effected no change in alcohol concentration over that found when alcohol was given alone. This indicates that the reputed antagonistic effect of caffeine and alcohol is not due to any destructive action of caffeine on alcohol.

Epinephrine and pituitrin.—The effects of a number of hormones other than insulin, notably epinephrine, pituitrin, and thyroxin, have received considerable attention. We have already seen that thyroxin is ineffective. Widmark (38) found epinephrine did not change the rate of alcohol metabolism in dogs, and Fleming and Reynolds (27) later confirmed this finding in man. Widmark (40) also obtained no effect from pituitrin. Blotner (72) investigated the blood alcohol curve after the administration of 0.6 cc. of alcohol per kilogram as a 20% solution in grape juice and water to fasting normal subjects and subjects with diabetes insipidus; the latter showed a sharper rise, higher maximum, and more rapid fall than the controls. When pituitrin was administered this abnormal curve returned toward the normal type. Interestingly enough, forcing fluids produced the same type of curve in normals as was seen in the subjects with diabetes insipidus, and again pituitrin was effective in returning it to the normal range. Since the alcohol was given by mouth, and since the type of curve shown by the subjects with diabetes insipidus was exactly what one would see with increased speed of absorption, it seems more than likely that it was this, rather than any direct action of pituitrin on alcohol metabolism, that was responsible.

Summary of alcohol metabolism.—It is possible, then, to summarize briefly our knowledge concerning the metabolism of alcohol. At least the initial step or steps in the combustion of alcohol can take place only in the liver, and is a specific function of an enzyme system in that organ. This stage proceeds no further than the production of acetic acid, and can be easily reproduced in vitro. Subsequently, and probably quite rapidly, for they have not been demonstrated in any quantities in the blood stream, the intermediary product or products are either burned to carbon dioxide and water in the tissues or are converted to other compounds which can either be burned or stored in the body. Whether or not one or the other, or both, of these processes takes place we have no direct knowledge. When glucose is not being burned, owing to either starvation or a high fat diet, the rate of alcohol metabolism is decreased disproportionately to metabolism in general. For a short period after the administration of protein or amino acids the rate of alcohol metabolism is accelerated. A more prolonged acceleration may be brought about by the administration of relatively large doses of insulin, either with or without glucose, while a considerable increase in body temperature is also effective in speeding up alcohol metabolism.

The rate of alcohol metabolism varies from species to species, generally in proportion to the basal metabolic rate. In the individual species it varies with the amount of functionally active liver tissue present. For all practical purposes it may be assumed that the rate of alcohol metabolism is relatively independent of the concentration in the tissues, although this is not absolutely true. Although prolonged imbibition of alcohol is not effective in significantly increasing the rate of alcohol metabolism, this evidence in no way refutes the existence of an acquired tolerance to alcohol.

Alcohol is capable of providing from 40 to 70% or more of the basal energy requirements in the homeothermic animal. Although the initial metabolic process must take place in the liver, and is unaffected in rate by activity or environmental temperature, there is no evidence to controvert the possibility of the intermediary products being available, either as such or after conversion to other compounds, for the production of muscular energy or heat. It is well to bear in mind that if we assume the disappearance from the body of alcohol indicates its combustion to carbon dioxide and water within a very short time, a concept which has been generally accepted, we cannot expect any therapeutic measure aimed at removal of alcohol by combustion to more than double its rate of disappearance, since any more rapid combustion of alcohol would provide more calories than the body could use, with an increase in total heat production, a situation that has not been shown to occur with alcohol.

REFERENCES

1. WIDMARK, E. M. P., "Die Maximalgrenzen der Alkoholkonsumption," *Biochem. Zeit.*, **259**:285, 1933
2. CARPENTER, T. M., "The Effect of Glucose on the Metabolism of Ethyl Alcohol in Man," *J. Pharmacol*, **60**:264, 1937
3. NICLOUX, M., "Combustion de l'alcool chez le poecilotherme; action de la température," *Compt. rend. soc. biol.*, **108**:17, 1931
4. NICLOUX, M., "Vitesse de réaction, quotient de température selon Van't Hoff et combustion de l'alcool dans l'organisme du poecilotherme," *Compt. rend. soc. biol.*, **108**:21, 1937
5. LEBRETON, E., "Pourcentage des oxydations couvert par l'alcool ethylique chez les poecilothermes," *Compt. rend. soc. biol.*, **122**:564, 1936
6. BATTELLI, F., and STERN, L., "Alcoholase in Animal Tissues," *Compt. rend. soc. biol.*, **67**:419, 1909
7. LEBRETON, E., "Microtechnic for Quantitative Study of Oxidation of Ethyl Alcohol in Tissues," *Compt. rend. soc. biol.*, **118**:64, 1935
8. NEWMAN, H. W., CUTTING, W. C., and TAINTER, M. L., "Action of Dinitrophenol on Rate of Oxidation of Ethyl Alcohol in Vitro," *Proc. Soc. Exp. Biol. and Med.*, **32**:1479, 1935
9. LELOIR, L. F., and MUNOZ, J. M., "Ethyl Alcohol Metabolism in Animal Tissues," *Biochem. J.*, **32**:299, 1938
10. REICHEL, L., and KOHLE, H., "Alcohol Dehydrogenase of Liver," *Hoppe-Seyler's Zeit. physiol. Chemie*, **236**:158, 1935
11. FEISSINGER, L., BENARD, H., COURTIAL, J., and DERMER, L., "Combustion de l'alcool éthylique au cours de la perfusion du foie," *Compt. rend. soc. biol.*, **122**:1255, 1936
12. LUNDSGAARD, E., "Alcohol Oxidation in Liver and Muscle," *Skand. Arch. Physiol.*, **77**:56, 1937
13. NEWMAN, H. W., VAN WINKLE, W., JR., KENNEDY, N. K., and MORTON, M. C., "Comparative Effects of Propylene Glycol, Other Glycols, and Alcohol on the Liver Directly," *J. Pharmacol.*, **68**:194, 1940
14. CHAPHEAU, M., "La combustion de l'alcool éthylique au cours de quelques intoxications," *Compt. rend. soc. biol.*, **116**:889, 1934
15. BROGGI, E., "Relationship between Experimental Lesions of the Liver and Behavior of the Alcoholemic Curve," *Rass. studi psichiat.*, **24**:579, 1935
16. ERWTEMAN, J., and HEERES, P. A., "Clinical and Experimental Observations about Alcohol-Tolerance," *Acta Med. Skand.*, **96**:198, 1938
17. MIRSKY, I. A., and NELSON, N., "The Influence of the Pancreas and the Liver on the Oxidation of Ethyl Alcohol," *Am. J. Physiol.*, **127**:308, 1939
18. NEWMAN, H. W., unpublished work, 1935
19. MELLANBY, E., *Alcohol: Its Absorption into and Disappearance from the Blood Stream under Different Conditions*, National Research Council (Great Britain) Special Report Series, No. 31, 1919
20. WIDMARK, E. M. P., "Distribution and Transformation of Ethyl Alcohol in the Dog," *Biochem. Zeit.*, **267**:128, 1933
21. HAGGARD, H. W., and GREENBERG, L. A., "Studies in the Absorption, Dis-

tribution, and Elimination of Ethyl Alcohol," *J. Pharmacol.*, **52**:150, 1934
22. Gabbe, E., "Über den Gehalt des Blutes am Alkohol nach intravenoser Injection desselben beim Menschen," *Deut. Arch. klin. Med.*, **122**:81, 1917
23. Mehrtens, H. G., and Newman, H. W., "Alcohol Injected Intravenously; Its Penetration into the Cerebrospinal Fluid in Man," *Arch. Neurol. Psychiatry*, **30**:1092, 1933
24. Haggard, H. W., and Greenberg, L. A., "Studies in the Absorption, Distribution, and Elimination of Alcohol. V. The Influence of Glycocol on the Absorption of Alcohol," *J. Pharmacol.*, **68**:482, 1940
25. Eggleton, M. G., "Some Factors Affecting the Metabolic Rate of Alcohol," *J. Physiol.*, **98**:239, 1940
26. Newman, H. W., and Cutting, W. C., "Alcohol Injected Intravenously; Rate of Disappearance from the Blood Stream in Man," *J. Pharmacol.*, **54**:371, 1935
27. Fleming, R., and Reynolds, D., "Experimental Studies in Alcoholism. IV. Attempts to Modify the Concentration of Alcohol in the Blood after Intravenous Administration of Alcohol," *J. Pharmacol.*, **54**:236, 1935
28. Fleming, R., and Stotz, E., "Experimental Studies in Alcoholism. II. The Alcohol Content of the Blood and Spinal Fluid Following Intravenous Administration of Alcohol in Chronic Alcoholism and the Psychoses," *Arch. Neurol. Psychiatry*, **35**:117, 1936
29. Jetter, W. J., "Studies in Alcohol. II. Experimental Feeding of Alcohol to Nonalcoholic Individuals," *Am. J. Med. Sci.*, **196**:487, 1938
30. Goldfarb, W., Bowman, K. M., and Parker, S., "The Treatment of Acute Alcoholism with Glucose and Insulin," *J. Clin. Investigation*, **18**:581, 1939
31. LeBreton, E., "La concentration de l'alcool ethylique dans le sang, permet-elle de conclure à sa vitesse d'oxydation dans l'organisme?" *Compt. rend. soc. biol.*, **117**:707, 1934
32. LeBreton, E., "Détermination comparée de la vitesse d'oxydation de l'alcool dans l'organisme par des courbes d'alcolémie et le dosage directe," *Compt. rend. soc. biol.*, **119**:568, 1935
33. LeBreton, E., "Influence de la concentration en alcool realisée au niveau des tissues sur la vitesse d'oxydation in vivo," *Compt. rend. soc. biol.*, **119**:572, 1935
34. Newman, H. W., Lehman, A. J., and Cutting, W. C., "Effect of Dosage on Rate of Disappearance of Alcohol from the Blood Stream," *J. Pharmacol.*, **61**:58, 1937
35. Eggleton, M. G., "Determination of the Metabolic Rate of Alcohol," *J. Physiol.*, **98**:228, 1940
36. Newman, H. W., "Determination of Ethyl Alcohol in Body Fluids," *J. Pharmacol.*, **56**:278, 1936
37. Newman, H. W., and Lehman, A. J., "Rate of Disappearance of Alcohol from the Blood Stream in Various Species," *Arch. intern. pharmacodynamie*, **55**:440, 1937
38. LeBreton, E., "Evolution de la vitesse d'oxydation de l'alcool éthylique

chez l'homeotherme au cours de la croissance," *Compt. rend. soc. biol.*, **122**:561, 1936

39. LEBRETON, E., NICLOUX, M., and SHAEFFER, G., "Coefficient of Ethyl Alcohol Oxidation and Basal Metabolism in Some Homeothermic Species," *Compt. rend. acad. sci.*, **200**:1133, 1935
40. WIDMARK, E. M. P., "Hormonal Einfluss auf den Alkoholumsatz," *Biochem. Zeit.*, **282**:79, 1935
41. HARGER, R. N., and HULPIEU, H. R., "The Effect of Certain Drugs on the Metabolism of Ethyl Alcohol," *J. Pharmacol*, **54**:145, 1935
42. WIDMARK, E. M. P., "Über die Einwirkung des Dinitrophenole auf die Umselzungsgeschwindigkeit des Athylalkohols," *Biochem. Zeit.*, **276**: 268, 1935
43. NEWMAN, H. W., and CUTTING, W. C., "The Action of Dinitrophenol and Insulin in Accelerating the Metabolism of Ethyl Alcohol," *J. Clin. Investigation*, **14**:945, 1935
44. NEWMAN, H. W., and TAINTER, M. L., "Effect of Dinitrophenol on Rate of Alcohol Metabolism," *J. Pharmacol.*, **57**:67, 1936
45. MCFARLAND, R. A., and BARACH, A. L., "The Relationship between Alcoholic Intoxication and Anoxemia," *Am. J. Med. Sci.*, **192**:186, 1936
46. NEWMAN, H. W., and CARD, J. F., "The Actual Value of Carbon Dioxide–Oxygen Inhalation in Accelerating the Reduction of Total Body Alcohol," *J. Am. Med. Assoc.*, **106**:595, 1936
47. CARPENTER, T. M., "Ethyl Alcohol in Fowls after Exposure to Alcohol Vapor," *J. Pharmacol.*, **37**:217, 1929
48. CARPENTER, T. M., LEE, R. C., and BURDETT, M., "The Effect of Muscular Exercise on the Disappearance of Ethyl Alcohol in Man," *Am. J. Physiol.* (*Proc.*), **105**:17, 1933
49. CANZANELLI, A., GUILD, R., and RAPPORT, D., "The Use of Ethyl Alcohol as a Fuel in Muscular Exercise," *Am. J. Physiol.*, **110**:416, 1934
50. NYMAN, E., and PALMLOV, A., "On the Effect of Muscular Exercise on the Metabolism of Ethyl Alcohol," *Skand. Arch. Physiol.*, **68**:271, 1934
51. LEBRETON, E., "Demonstration directe de la non-utilisation de l'alcool éthylique comme source d'énergie pour le travail musculaire du rat," *Compt. rend. soc. biol.*, **118**:62, 1935
52. CARPENTER, T. M., "The Effect of Fructose on the Metabolism of Ethyl Alcohol in Man," *J. Pharmacol.*, **60**:286, 1937
53. LEBRETON, E., "Signification physiologique de l'oxydation de l'alcool éthylique dans l'organisme," *Compt. rend. soc. biol.*, **122**:566, 1936
54. LEBRETON, E., "Influence du froid sur la vitesse de l'alcool éthylique chez l'homeotherme," *Compt. rend. soc. biol.*, **116**:82, 1934
55. WIDMARK, E. M. P., "Über die Einwirkung von Aminosauren auf den Alkoholgehalt des Blutes," *Biochem. Zeit.*, **265**:237, 1933
56. LEBRETON, E., "Influence de la nature de l'aliment brulé sur la vitesse d'oxydation de l'alcool dans l'organisme," *Compt. rend. soc. biol.*, **117**:709, 1934
57. NEWMAN, H. W., unpublished data, 1935
58. GOLDFARB, W., and BOWMAN, K. M., "The Effect of Glucose on the Oxi-

dation of Alcohol in Vitro," *Proc. Soc. Exp. Biol. and Med.*, **39**:471, 1938
59. Chapheau, M., "Action de la phlorizine et de l'acide iodoacétique sur la combustion de l'alcool éthylique chez le lapin," *Compt. rend. soc. biol.*, **116**:887, 1934
60. Bickel, A., "The Biologic Effect of Alcohol on Metabolism," Foreign Letters (Berlin), *J. Am. Med. Assoc.*, **106**:2171, 1936
61. Newman, H. W., unpublished data, 1932, 1936
62. Constantin, J. D., "General Anesthesia by Intravenous Injection of Ethyl Alcohol," *Lancet*, **1**:1247, 1929
63. Carpenter, T. M., "The Effect of Galactose on the Metabolism of Ethyl Alcohol in Man," *J. Pharmacol.*, **60**:254, 1937
64. Clark, B. B., and Morrissey, R. W., "Influence of Insulin, Glucose, and Alkalizing Salts on the Rate of Disappearance of Alcohol from the Blood," *Am. J. Physiol.*, **123**:37, 1938
65. Supniewski, J. V., "The Influence of Insulin on the Acetaldehyde Formation in the Body of Animals," *J. Biol. Chem.*, **70**:13, 1926
66. Hirschfelder, A. D., and Maxwell, H. C., "Effect of Insulin in Experimental Intoxication with Alcohol and Acetone," *Am. J. Physiol.*, **70**:520, 1924
67. Goldfarb, W., and Wortis, J., "The Availability of Ethyl Alcohol for Human Brain Oxidations," *Quart. J. Stud. Alcohol*, **1**:268, 1940
68. Serianni, E., "Action of Insulin on Alcoholism Induced in a Normal Person," *Atti. accad. Lincei*, **21**:394, 1935
69. Carr, C. J., Schmidt, J. E., Harne, W., and Krantz, J. C., Jr., "The Influence of Insulin-Free Pancreatic Extract on the Gaseous Exchange of the White Rat," *J. Pharmacol.*, **50**:151, 1934
70. Lehman, A. J., and Newman, H. W., "Propylene Glycol: Rate of Metabolism, Absorption, and Excretion, with a Method for Estimation in Body Fluids," *J. Pharmacol.*, **60**:312, 1937
71. Clark, B. B., Morrissey, R. W., and Fazekas, J. F., "Insulin and the Oxidation of Alcohol by Excised Diabetic Liver Tissue," *Science*, **88**:285, 1938
72. Blotner, H., "Alcohol Tolerance Tests in Normal Individuals and in Patients with Diabetes Mellitus and Diabetes Insipidus," *New Engl. J. Med.*, **220**:283, 1939
73. Wortis, J., Bowman, K. M., and Goldfarb, W., "The Use of Insulin in the Treatment of Alcoholism," *Med. Clin. North America*, **24**:671, 1940
74. LeBreton, E., "Influence du jeûne sur la vitesse d'oxydation de l'alcool éthylique chez le rat blanc," *Compt. rend. soc. biol.*, **122**:330, 1936
75. Addis, T., Poo, L. J., and Lew, W., "The Quantities of Protein Lost by the Various Organs and Tissues of the Body during a Fast," *J. Biol. Chem.*, **115**:111, 1936
76. Addis, T., Poo, L. J., and Lew, W., "Protein Lost from Liver during a 2 Day Fast," *J. Biol. Chem.*, **115**:117, 1936
77. Addis, T., Poo, L. J., and Lew, W., "The Rate of Protein Formation in the Organs and Tissues of the Body," *J. Biol. Chem.*, **116**:343, 1936
78. Dontcheff, L., "Evolution de la vitesse d'oxydation de l'alcool éthylique

au cours du jeûne chez le rat blanc," *Compt. rend. soc. biol.*, **126:** 462, 1937

79. Dontcheff, L., "Influence de divers types d'aliment sur la vitesse d'oxydation de l'alcool éthylique chez l'homeotherme inanitié (rat blanc)," *Compt. rend. soc. biol.*, **126**:465, 1937
80. Gettler, A. O., "Chemical Evidences of Alcoholic Intoxication and Their Medico-Legal Significance," *New Engl. J. Med.*, **201**:725, 1929
81. Fleming, R., and Stotz, E., "Alcohol Content of Blood and Spinal Fluid after Oral Administration in Chronic Alcoholism and the Psychoses," *Arch. Neurol. Psychiatry*, **33**:492, 1935
82. Levy, J., "Alcoholisme experimentale, fixation de l'alcool sur les tissus de l'organisme accoûtumé à cette substance," *Bull. soc. chim. biol.*, **17**:27, 1935
83. Newman, H. W., and Lehman, A. J., "Nature of Acquired Tolerance to Ethyl Alcohol," *J. Pharmacol.*, **62**:301, 1938
84. Newman, H. W., and Cutting, W. C., "Alcohol Injected Intravenously: Effect of Habituation on Rate of Metabolism," *J. Pharmacol.*, **55**:82, 1935
85. Newman, H. W., and Cutting, W. C., "Alcohol Injected Intravenously: Further Observations on the Effect of Habituation on Rate of Metabolism," *J. Pharmacol.*, **57**:388, 1936
86. Gettler, A. O., and Freireich, A. W., "The Nature of Alcohol Tolerance," *Am. J. Surg.*, **27**:328, 1935
87. Koopmann, H., and Kempski, H., "Observations on the Influence of the Consumption of Coffee on the Alcohol Content of the Blood, and Forensic Value of the Alcohol Concentration of the Urine," *Münch. med. Wochschr.*, **84**:780, 1937

PART TWO

TOXICOLOGY OF ETHYL ALCOHOL

CHAPTER IV

ACUTE TOXICITY

That the important toxic effect of ethyl alcohol, at least in the phylum chordata, is on the central nervous system, there can be no doubt. Repeated investigations have demonstrated that concentrations sufficient to bring about significant changes in the functions of other systems exceed those tolerated by the nervous system.

In any consideration of the acutely fatal dose of an agent there are a number of factors that must be taken into consideration. In the first place, we must be assured of the purity of the preparation; and in this particular ethyl alcohol presents little difficulty, as it is readily obtainable in essentially pure form. Thus we can be sure that the toxic action is due to alcohol itself, and not to some impurity. Since it is a reasonable assumption that the toxic action on the nervous system is dependent on access of the agent to nervous tissue, it follows that the route of administration may be of considerable importance in determining the fatal dose, as must also be the rate of administration, since we have seen that alcohol may be both metabolized and eliminated from the body.

Effect on central nervous system.—The subjective appreciation of the effect of alcohol in man is such that, until objective investigation of the action of the drug on the central nervous system produced evidence to the contrary, alcohol enjoyed the reputation of being a cerebral stimulant; and even in our present enlightened day such is its reputation to the laity. However, a great mass of work, mainly concerned with tests of a psychological nature, has quite conclusively demonstrated that the action of significant concentrations of alcohol on the central nervous system is one of depression and later paralysis of function. This work is too well known to warrant review by us. There has, however, recently been some experimental work which casts some degree of doubt on the universality of this dictum so far as application to all parts of the nervous system is concerned. Thus Masserman and Jacobson (1) determined the excitability of the cerebral cortex and the hypothalamus of the cat, in both acute and recovery preparations, after the administration of alcohol both locally and systemically, under ether anesthesia. They placed their electrodes by means of the Horsley-Clarke stereotaxic apparatus, using electrical stimulation, and determining the cortical threshold by means of the appearance of movement and the hypothalamic threshold by the presence of emotional mimetic responses. They found that while 0.06% and above of alcohol injected directly into either location produced definite depression of function, 0.02% was slightly stimulating. On the other hand, intravenous (systemic) injection of 1 to 2 cc. of alcohol per kilogram depressed the electrical excitability of the cortex, although it had little effect, or even a stimulating effect, on the hypothalamus. That the latter effect might be due not to direct stimulation but rather to removal of cortical inhibition by depressant action of the alcohol on the cortex was recognized by the authors. Using the same technic in unanesthetized cats, Masserman (2) found that electrical reactivity of the hypothalamus, as judged by the rage reaction, was increased by direct injection of .01% alcohol in Ringer's solution but was not materially changed by intraperitoneal injection of 0.5 to 1.0 cc. per kilogram of alcohol. On the contrary, the responses of the posterior sigmoid cortex were not affected by such direct injections but were augmented after intraperitoneal alcohol injections of 1.0 cc. per kilogram. Ether anesthesia was thus effective in abolishing the effect on the cortex, while not affecting that on the hypothalamus. From this he concluded that small amounts of alcohol may facilitate the reactivity of the central nervous system, especially of the diencephalic centers. It seems to us that certain of the discrepancies between the effects of systemic and of local injections of alcohol in this work may be explicable on the basis of the concentrations employed by the two routes. No doubt the local injections, which were of a concentration of 0.01 to 0.02%, were further diluted by the tissues into which they were injected. On the other hand, with the intraperitoneal and intravenous injection of doses of 1.0 cc. per kilogram we should expect tissue concentrations up to 0.1%, which exceeds the concentration found by Masserman and Jacobson (1) to be depressant for both cortical and hypothalamic centers. The upshot of the work is that, while concentrations of alcohol met with in individuals suspected of intoxication are generally conceded to be depressant for the central nervous system, there is some evidence to indicate that very low concentrations may have some stimulating activity and that this activity seems to be more pronounced in the lower centers than in the cerebral cortex.

In man, it has been amply demonstrated that even low concentrations of alcohol are accompanied by depression of function of the central nervous system. This has recently been demonstrated quantitatively by Bahnsen and Vedel-Petersen (3) and by Newman and Fletcher (4), with whose work we shall concern ourselves more in detail when we consider the effect of alcohol on the driving of motor vehicles.

Nystagmus.—Bernhard and Goldberg (5) have called attention to the presence of nystagmus, both vertical and horizontal, in acute alcoholic intoxication, a phenomenon which we have seen in the dog as well as in man. They explain this on the basis of a paralytic action on the cerebellum.

Conditioned reflexes.—Efforts have been made to make use of the conditioned reflex technic to demonstrate the effect of alcohol on cortical function. Avdeyev (6), using a single dog, induced both positive and negative conditioned reflexes. When these were well established, he gave both small doses, consisting of 30 to 100 cc. of 10% alcohol, and large doses of 100 to 250 cc., and determined the reflex responses. There was consistently found an inhibition of both the positive and negative conditioned responses. When alcohol was administered daily for 5 to 10 days, a period of a week or more was required before the conditioned reflexes returned to the normal level. Gantt (7) conducted similar experiments with 5 dogs with well-established conditioned reflexes. Alcohol was given in doses of 0.5, 1.5, and 3 to 4 cc. per kilogram of 95% given with an equal volume of milk and diluted to 20% strength with water. This mixture the dogs would drink voluntarily with a little coaxing. There was no change in the ordinary behavior of the animals with the 0.5 cc. dose. With the 1.5 cc. dose they showed some incoordination and depression of consciousness, while with the 3 and 4 cc. doses marked drunkenness was evident. The reflexes were tested from 10 to 90 minutes after administration of the alcohol. In addition to the conditioned reflexes, which take place at a cortical level, the unconditioned reflexes were tested as well. The factor which was considered to be of importance was the ratio of reduction of the conditioned reflex to the reduction of the unconditioned reflex. This was expressed as a percentage. Above 100% indicated a cortical effect, below this figure a subcortical effect. In normal dogs the 0.5 cc. dose gave no cortical effect (101%), while the 1.5 cc. dose gave a ratio of 126%, indicating some degree of cortical depression, and the 3 and 4 cc. doses gave a ratio of 297%, or marked cortical depression. In one of the dogs, which had previously had half its cortex removed, even the smallest dose produced definite evidence of cortical depression. In no case was any stimulant effect of alcohol evident, and in the individual dog the effect was proportional to the dose. There was, however, considerable variation between the different animals at the same dosage, the more stable animals showing the least effect. An important fact well demonstrated by these experiments was that nervous function at the higher, or cortical, level was much more affected by alcohol than at the lower, subcortical level.

Motility during sleep.—Further evidence of the depressant effect of alcohol on the nervous system was obtained by Mullin, Kleitman, and Cooperman (8) in their studies of the effect of alcohol on motility during sleep. Using a recording device attached to the bed capable of registering the movements of the subject during sleep, they compared such records obtained from 8 male subjects after administration of 60 to 75 cc. of 95% alcohol diluted to 19% 45 minutes to 1 hour before retiring and after administration of a similar volume of water as a control. The subjects, who were abstainers or occasional drinkers, all fell asleep immediately when alcohol was given. Some complained of headache the morning after. In but one case was there any change in the total motility during the night, and in that case there was an increase of 16%. However, if the night was divided into a first and second half, a consistent difference became apparent. In the alcohol experiments, there was a decrease in motility during the first half of the night, with an increase during the second half sufficient to make the total motility equal to the controls. Also the number of times the subject awakened during the night was decreased by alcohol. In explanation of these findings we should like to point out that the amount of alcohol ingested by these subjects would be completely eliminated from the body in not more than six hours, and that during the last two hours of this period the blood alcohol level would be quite low. Thus it is evident that during the period when an appreciable concentration of alcohol existed in the blood, motility was definitely decreased. The increase in motility during the second half of the night was no doubt due to the onset of post-alcoholic symptoms generally termed the "hangover," the exact cause of which is obscure.

These authors also noted a decrease in body temperature after ingestion of alcohol. That this was ascribable to increased heat loss due to cutaneous vasodilation was nicely shown by the fact that if the environmental temperature was slightly above body temperature such a decrease did not occur.

Intoxication and anoxia.—The mechanism by which alcohol depresses the function of the nervous system is not clear. The similarity between the symptoms of alcoholic intoxication and anoxia has been remarked by a number of observers, notably by McFarland and Barach (9). They tested 23 human subjects with doses of alcohol from ¾ to 1¼ gm. per kilogram by mouth, administering 6 psychological tests both in air and in an atmosphere of 50% oxygen and 2% carbon dioxide. In 75% of the subjects there was an improvement in performance with the administration of oxygen after alcohol, but no control observations of possible improvement in subjects without alcohol under similar conditions were made. Interestingly, they found that the rise in blood lactic-acid concentration known to occur after ingestion of alcohol was not nearly so marked in those experiments in which the subjects breathed 50% oxygen. It was not stated whether the incidence of hangovers, thought to be related to the increased blood lactic-acid concentration, was less in the oxygen experiments than when air was breathed. Such a study would be of some interest. Whether the improvement in performance of the psychological tests when oxygen was administered should be interpreted as evidence of the depression brought about by alcohol being due to interference with cerebral oxidative processes which can be combated by oxygen administration or to the somewhat lower blood alcohol concentrations noted in 80% of the subjects, it is not possible to decide on the evidence presented.

That oxygen administration is ineffective in overcoming the depression of the respiratory center responsible for death from respiratory paralysis when alcohol is administered in constantly increasing amounts has been demonstrated by Haggard *et al.* (10). They determined the concentration of alcohol in the jugular blood of rats at the time respiratory paralysis occurred after injection of small repeated doses of alcohol by the intraperitoneal route. This concentration was 9.30 mg. per cubic centimeter in rats breathing air and 9.29 mg. per cubic centimeter in rats breathing oxygen.

Metabolism of alcohol by the brain.—There is no good direct evidence that alcohol can be metabolized by brain tissue; as a matter of fact it is generally accepted that only glucose can subserve this function. Indirect evidence that alcohol cannot substitute for glucose in cerebral metabolism was obtained by Goldfarb and Wortis (11). They administered 200 cc. of 25% alcohol by mouth, and in one case 50 cc. of 10% alcohol intravenously, to 11 patients in hypoglycemic coma incidental to insulin shock therapy. In one of the cases there was slight evidence of arousal; the others remained the same or sank deeper in coma. They point out the possibility, which seems remote to us, that this is not conclusive proof that alcohol cannot be burned by the brain, as the presence of glucose may be necessary for such oxidation to take place, as evidenced by the catalytic effect of glucose on alcohol oxidation in vitro.

Effect on cerebral metabolism.—Wortis, Bowman, and Goldfarb (12, 13) have shown a decrease in cerebral oxygen consumption in acute alcoholic intoxication. They estimated the cerebral oxygen consumption and carbon-dioxide production by the arterio-venous difference method, using venous blood from the internal jugular vein and arterial blood from the brachial or femoral artery, and estimating blood flow from determination of systemic circulation time. The cerebral oxygen difference was significantly lower than normal in the majority of cases in alcoholic coma, indicating a lessened cerebral metabolism. The respiratory quotient remained in the vicinity of 1.0, which is against the metabolism of alcohol by the brain, since alcohol has a respiratory quotient of 0.67. They confirmed the presence of increased lactic-acid concentrations in the blood of alcoholics, finding up to 39 mg.% as against 19 mg.% in normal subjects.

Wortis (14) had previously attacked the problem by the Warburg technic in vitro. He found that in the presence of alcohol the respiratory quotient of rat brain was 0.93, which he concluded was evidence of metabolism by the brain of a small amount of alcohol. On inspection of the data, however, we see that in the rats given 50 cc. 19% alcohol per kilogram before sacrifice, in one case the respiratory quotient was .93 and in another .95, while a cat getting 2.5 cc. per kilogram intravenously had a respiratory quotient of .975. The same range of values was obtained for illuminating gas, which is certainly not metabolized by the brain; so that the case for alcohol being burned by brain tissue is not a strong one.

Alcohol and vision.—There have been attempts in man to demonstrate the depressant effects of alcohol on the nervous system by testing its effect on the organs of special senses. Thus Colson (15), his attention called to the problem by a recollection of having at one time had an attack of tunnel vision after imbibition of alcohol and on another occasion of noticing night blindness after a cocktail party, tested visual acuity, near vision, color vision, visual fields, muscle balance, and dark adaptation in 21 subjects after ingestion of alcohol. The subjects, who ranged in age from 21 to 44 years, received 2 ounces of whisky with soda water at half-hourly intervals, the total dose in most cases being 8 to 10 ounces, although some hardy souls got up to 20 ounces. There was no attempt to determine blood alcohol concentrations. No effect on visual acuity, near vision, or visual fields was demonstrated. If dark adaptation was originally normal, it did not change; but in those subjects with impaired dark adaptation it got worse. There was a shift in muscle balance, some subjects who were exophoric without alcohol becoming esophoric. In the face of these results, how Dr. Colson explained his own earlier subjective experiences is not evident.

Newman and Fletcher (16) tested visual acuity, visual fields, muscle balance, dark adaptation, depth perception, and hearing in a group of 50 individuals before and after approximately 1 cc. of whisky per pound of body weight. Significant changes in visual acuity and fields were noted, while muscle balance showed changes similar to those noted by Colson (15). Depth perception, tested by both the Army rod test and the Keystone Telebinocular instrument, was definitely impaired in most subjects, with considerable individual variation not related to the blood alcohol concentration achieved. Audiometer readings indicated no change in most individuals. As with Colson, those subjects having poor dark adaptation became in general worse after alcohol. On the other hand, those with normal function showed, in about half the cases, a definite improvement after alcohol.

Alcohol and dark adaptation.—This effect on dark adaptation is in accord with the findings of Pett (17), who noted a shortened recovery time from glare in some of his subjects and on questioning them found that they had taken alcohol the night before. This effect, which amounted to about a 45% reduction, was maximal at 24 and 48 hours after imbibition and returned to normal by the seventh day. This correlates well with the conclusions of Clausten *et al.* (18, 19). They gave 60 cc. of alcohol as a 20% solution to each of 8 dogs and determined the vitamin A content of their blood, finding a maximum increase at 7 and 24 hours after ingestion of the alcohol. Alcohol administered by intravenous or portal injection produced the same result, which they believed to be a mobilization of vitamin A from the liver brought about by the action of alcohol on that organ. They confirmed their findings in man, administering alcohol as mixed drinks during the evening, the average dose being one cubic centimeter per pound. They took blood samples 4 and 12 hours after the first drink, and found in all cases a slight increase in circulating vitamin A. Thus the effect of alcohol on dark adaptation is an indirect one, brought about by mobilization of vitamin A. It is not surprising that in those individuals showing defective dark adaptation, indicative of vitamin A deficiency, no change or even a decrease in dark adaptation may result from alcohol.

Effects of different alcoholic beverages.—There is an impression among the laity that various alcoholic beverages vary considerably in their toxicity, in a manner unrelated to their alcoholic content. In certain cases this is undoubtedly true, when other toxic agents form a part of the beverage, as in beer (lupulin) and absinthe (wormwood) for instance. Other than in these special beverages, however, it is almost certain that the toxicity is entirely proportional to alcoholic content and that the lay impression is ascribable to differences in absorbability and the local effects on the gastric and intestinal mucosa of other constituents of the mixtures.

Those studies which have been made of the toxicity of different types of alcoholic beverages have shown little difference between them. Muehlberger (20) studied the effects of synthetic ethyl alcohol made from ethylene derived from the "cracking" of petroleum, and of grain fermentation alcohol, as well as of blended whiskies compounded by the mixing of equal parts of straight Bourbon whisky, four years old, with each of the two types of alcohol so diluted as to maintain the concentration of alcohol in the whisky at its former level. Fifteen male subjects were used, varying in age from 22 to 51 years. Of the two types of alcohol, the abstainers were given 0.5 cc. per kilogram, moderate drinkers 1.0 cc. per kilogram, and heavy drinkers 1.5 cc. per kilogram, all as a 10% solution in cool water ingested at a constant rate over a period of 30 minutes. Each subject received both types of alcohol. Urine specimens were secured at 45, 90, 120, 180, and 240 minutes after ingestion. The peak of urine alcohol concentration—which averaged 90 mg.% for the abstainers, 125 mg.% for the moderate drinkers, and 165 mg.% for the heavy drinkers—as well as the acme of inebriation both occurred at 45 minutes. All degrees of intoxication from "a feeling of fullness in the head to a drunken stupor" were experienced, but no attempt was made to correlate the degree of drunkenness with the urine alcohol concentration. There was absolutely no difference in the response to the two types of alcohol. The same was found to be true of the two blended whiskies, even so far as the incidence and severity of hangovers was concerned.

Barlow (21), using the same array of beverages, covered a wider field of investigation. Local irritant effects and the effects on the frog heart and on the earthworm were not different for the various preparations. Administered intraperitoneally to rats, the whiskies were more toxic than either alcohol alone, undoubtedly owing to the presence of substances other than alcohol which might be expected to be poorly tolerated by this route of administration. When given as the sole source of fluid to rats over an extended period, both alcohols in 7.5% concentration did not affect the normal growth curve, but 15% definitely reduced it. Whisky diluted to the same strengths, however, increased the expected growth curve 19% at a concentration of 7.5% and showed no effect at 15%, thus showing to better advantage than the pure alcohols. Rabbits were given, by the oral route, 6.0 to 9.5 gm. per kilogram of alcohol, using the several preparations all adjusted to a final alcohol concentration of 30%. The symptoms of intoxication were similar in all cases, but the period of recovery was from 5 to 8 hours longer with whisky than with alcohol. Deaths occurring early were equal with whisky and alcohol, but late deaths were more frequent with whisky. In the cat, straight whisky was productive of more emesis and gastritis than were the other beverages, synthetic alcohol being the least objectionable in this regard. On intravenous administration to rabbits of 5 to 6 gm. per kilogram as a 30% solution in 28 to 40 minutes, again early deaths were equal with alcohol and whisky but late deaths were more numerous with whisky. In a group of 12 medical students no difference in effect of the various beverages on gastric secretion or gastric motility was found. In brief, the difference in toxicity of grain alcohol, synthetic alcohol, straight whisky, and the blended whiskies was of doubtful significance.

Acutely fatal dose in man.—There are very few valid data available on the acutely fatal dose of alcohol in man. Gettler (22), who has had a wide experience with autopsy material in which alcoholism was at least a factor in the fatal outcome, has said: "There is no definite amount of alcohol that one can say is a fatal dose." Gettler and Freireich (23) have reported a blood alcohol concentration of 1.032%, indicative of consumption of at least a quart and a half of whisky by a man of average weight. This figure is, however, far out of line with the present concept of lethal blood alcohol concentrations, and it is fairly well accepted that any concentration above 0.5% may result in death. Thus Jetter (24) reported two cases with 470 mg.% and 480 mg.% who died, with confirmation of the diagnosis of acute alcoholism at autopsy. This concentration could be attained in a person of average weight who drank approximately a pint and a half of whisky rapidly on an empty stomach. The fact that death from acute alcoholism does not occur more often is dependent on two things: First, it is unusual for an individual to imbibe a very large amount of alcohol rapidly under conditions favorable to its absorption, with the result that, under circumstances of the usual nature, imbibition and absorption are slow enough for the depressant effect on the central nervous system to keep pace with ingestion, and since coma occurs at considerably below the lethal concentration the individual stops drinking perforce before he ingests a dose sufficient to kill him. In the second place, even if, through some unusual circumstances, a large amount of alcohol is ingested on an empty stomach, the chances that it will be eliminated by emesis are quite good. The combination of these factors works so efficiently that when death does occur in acute alcoholism it is almost invariably ascribable to some other cause, the alcohol being merely a contributory, if admittedly a very important, factor.

Emetic action.—The emetic action of alcohol has not received the study which it deserves. The more generally accepted view is that it is incidental to local action on the gastric or intestinal mucosa, and undoubtedly this is to some extent correct. It does not, however, explain the observation of Kantarovich and Constantinovich (25), who report emesis in one subject after the administration of alcohol by the intravenous route. This observation had previously been made by Mehrtens and Newman (26) in four of a series of subjects given 1.0 cc. of alcohol per kilogram intravenously. These authors had shown (27) that under such circumstances the alcohol concentration in the gastric contents was not over 0.1%, which would hardly be expected to exert a locally irritant action. Thus we must conclude that at least part of the emetic action of alcohol is not due to local irritation. Whether this component of the emetic action is a truly central one, or is mediated reflexly from some other situation, cannot be answered without further investigation.

Acutely fatal dose in animals.—Because of the factors influencing absorption and distribution of alcohol in the animal body, dealt with at length in preceding chapters, it is obvious that the lethal dose of alcohol must be dependent on the route and speed of administration. Thus the gastric administration of alcohol to an animal in which the gastrointestinal tract is always full of food, as the rabbit, must result in such slow absorption of alcohol as to require a much larger dose than if the substance were administered by rapid intravenous injection, in which case delay in equilibration throughout the tissues would result in a blood alcohol concentration, and consequently a brain alcohol concentration, considerably exceeding that prevailing in the body as a whole. In spite of these variables there is a fair degree of agreement in the literature regarding the fatal dose of alcohol in experimental animals. Thus Munch and Schwartz (28) gave alcohol to rabbits by stomach tube and found the minimal narcotic dose, which they defined as that producing light narcosis in 50% of the animals, to be 5.5 cc. per kilogram, and the certain lethal dose—that producing death in all animals within 24 hours—to be 12.5 cc. per kilogram. Lehman and Newman (29) worked with the same animal but administered the alcohol intravenously at a constant rate of 0.5 cc. of 20% alcohol in normal saline per minute; they found the minimal anesthetic dose, producing corneal anesthesia, to be 5.6 gm. per kilogram, and the minimal lethal dose, producing stoppage of the heart, to be 9.4 gm. per kilogram. It was felt that the slowness of the injection (requiring about two hours) was sufficient to allow equilibration to keep pace with injection, which is borne out by the rather close agreement with the previous work with gastric administration of alcohol. It is probable that the somewhat higher lethal dose by the gastric route can be explained by slow absorption, with resultant destruction of a considerable quantity of alcohol in the body during the longer period necessary to attain the lethal concentration.

Species differences.—There is little doubt that the acutely fatal dose of alcohol varies with the species. Thus we have seen that Jetter (24) found a blood alcohol concentration of 470 and 480 mg.% in two men dying of acute alcoholic intoxication, a concentration that could be reached by parenteral administration of 5 cc. per kilogram. Haggard *et al.* (30) found the lethal dose for rats on repeated intraperitoneal injection to be 7.75 gm. per kilogram, while Lehman and Newman (29) reported 9.4 gm. per kilogram as the lethal dose for rabbits on intravenous injection, and Newman (31) has observed fatalities in dogs on intravenous injection at this same rate of doses as low as 6.0 cc. per kilogram. It seems probable that these differences in dosage cannot be wholly ascribed to variation in route and rate of administration, but rather are indicative of species differences in tolerance to alcohol.

Depression of respiratory center.—Haggard *et al.* (30) have attacked the problem from a different, and possibly more productive, angle. Acute deaths from alcohol are due to paralysis of respiration, the heart continuing to beat for some time after respiration ceases. From this they reasoned that the concentration of alcohol in the respiratory center was the important factor to investigate, since it was this concentration rather than that prevailing at any other location that produced paralysis of respiration and death. Since it is not feasible to determine directly the concentration of alcohol in the respiratory center, an indirect appraisal of this concentration must be made, and the best source of material was thought to be the venous blood from the brain. Especially during the period of active absorption there is a considerable difference in alcohol concentration in blood from different sources, for which reason the alcohol concentration of the respiratory center cannot be approximated by analysis of venous blood returning from an extremity, or even of arterial blood. The blood in the internal jugular vein should, however, indicate rather accurately the average alcohol concentration of the brain. True, it will be lower than those parts of the brain having a large blood flow and higher than those with a small blood flow; but if administration of alcohol is not too rapid the concentration of alcohol in internal jugular blood quite accurately reflects the concentration in the respiratory center. This is shown by the fact that under these conditions of relatively slow administration there is little difference between the concentration in arterial blood and that in jugular blood. Since the concentration in the respiratory center must lie between these values, the more nearly equal they are the more nearly must jugular concentration follow brain concentration; and it is for this reason that repeated small intraperitoneal injections were used in this study.

The authors make use of this variation in blood alcohol concentration of arterial and jugular blood during absorption of alcohol to explain an observation of Mellanby's (32) which they quote erroneously. They say: "he noted that the signs of intoxication were less marked for any given concentration of alcohol in the capillary blood (essentially the same as arterial) during the time the concentration was rising than when declining." They argue that, the concentration in the jugular blood being less than that in the arterial blood during the period of increment, the arterial (capillary) blood alcohol values obtained by Mellanby during this time really indicated a lower jugular concentration, and consequently a lower brain alcohol, than during the period of decline, when the two concentrations are much more nearly equal. This would very nicely explain the statement attributed by them to Mellanby. Unfortunately, they have made an error in their quotation. Mellanby actually said (31): "A dog begins to show signs of intoxication when the blood reaches about 354 cm. per 100 grammes of blood. . . . . When the alcohol has declined again to 354 cm. the dog will probably appear almost normal, and will certainly be less intoxicated than at a corresponding point on the ascent of the curve." Thus Haggard's explanation is a good one, but it explains the situation opposite to that which actually prevails, as we can confirm the true observation of Mellanby as above quoted, both in experimental animals and from personal subjective experience. The explanation of this phenomenon, which has been inadequately investigated, is obscure. Mellanby suggested that it may be due to an inability of the nervous system to accommodate itself to the rapidly increasing concentration of alcohol, an accommodation that ultimately takes place when the alcohol has been present for some time in essentially the same concentration.

To return to our consideration of the acutely fatal dose of alcohol, Haggard *et al.* (30) administered alcohol intraperitoneally to adult male rats, fasted for 16 hours. The alcohol was administered as a 50% solution, the initial injection being 3 gm. per kilogram. At the end of 30 minutes a further injection of 1 gm. per kilogram was given, at 45 and 60 minutes 0.25 gm., and thereafter 0.125 gm. each five minutes until respiratory failure ensued. A tracheotomy was performed in all cases to eliminate mechanical respiratory embarrassment, all animals were subjected to autopsy, and those showing evidence of disease were rejected. A sample of blood from the internal jugular vein was obtained at the time of respiratory failure and the alcohol concentration determined. The determination was made on 300 animals, of which 64 were discarded because of detection of respiratory infection at autopsy. The average concentration of alcohol in the jugular blood was 9.3 mg. per cubic centimeter, with an extreme range of 8.9 to 10.0 mg. per cubic centimeter. That this is very close to the actual concentration prevailing in the respiratory center at the moment of paralysis is borne out by the fact that spreading the injections out over a longer period did not change the lethal concentration.

Effects of various agents on lethal concentration.—By this same technic, Haggard *et al.* (10) investigated the effect of various agents on the concentration of alcohol necessary to produce respiratory arrest. Oxygen was ineffective, rats breathing such an atmosphere succumbing at a concentration of 9.29 mg. per cubic centimeter as against 9.30 for controls in air. Carbon dioxide, however, raised the lethal concentration to 10.3 mg. per cubic centimeter. The action here is no doubt due to the well-known stimulating action of carbon dioxide on the respiratory center offsetting a certain amount of the depression due to the alcohol. The effect was equal with carbon dioxide in air and in oxygen. Caffeine, dinitrophenol, benzedrine, acetanilid, phenacetine, antipyrine, and aspirin had no effect, while morphine in a dose of 5 mg. per kilogram reduced the lethal concentration to 8.12 mg. per cubic centimeter, and doses of 10 and 20 mg. per kilogram further reduced it to 7.74 and 7.39 mg. per cubic centimeter. From this they concluded that morphine was an undesirable sedative in the treatment of acute alcoholism.

Strychnine and barbiturates.—Strychnine they found ineffective in changing the lethal concentration, a finding in accord with the work of Gold and Travell (33). Not in accord with previous reports was their observation that doses of amytal from 5 to 50 mg. per kilogram did not change the concentration of alcohol at which death occurred. Except for some inadequately controlled work by Carriere, Huriez, and Willoquet (34), who reported that the intravenous injection of alcohol prevented death from otherwise fatal doses of a barbiturate (gardenal), the experimental evidence has been all in favor of a synergistic action of alcohol and the barbiturates. Thus Olszycka (35) gave graduated doses of alcohol and ethylbutylbarbiturate to mice and noted the resultant duration of sleep. Subthreshold doses of the two depressants when administered simultaneously gave periods of sleep up to 78 minutes, while with effective doses the sleeping time was much greater than the sum of the effects of each alone, the potentiation being most notable with the smaller doses. She repeated this work using rats (36), with which animals she was also able to determine the blood and brain alcohol concentrations at intervals of from 5 to 270 minutes after administration of the drugs, as well as in control animals. The potentiation was again evident, but the simultaneous administration of the barbiturate had no effect on the blood or brain alcohol concentrations, showing conclusively that the effect was a true pharmacological potentiation and was not due to any disturbance of distribution or metabolism of alcohol. Dille and Ahlquist reported similar findings (37) in rabbits. They performed 120 experiments on 48 rabbits, giving the alcohol as a 20% and the barbiturate (pentobarbital) as a 1% solution, both intravenously. The "sleeping time," gauged by the absence of the righting reflex, was 2 minutes with a dose of 10 mg. per kilogram of pentobarbital, 15 minutes with 15 mg. per kilogram, and 21 minutes with 20 mg. per kilogram, the rate of injection in all cases being 10 cc. per minute. With each of the three doses, alcohol, even in doses as low as 0.8 gm. per kilogram, gave marked potentiation, which was, however, greatest with the smaller doses. Blood alcohol concentration was followed for a period of 30 minutes, and no effect of the pentobarbital on its course was discernible. The authors concluded that there exists a potentiated synergism between pentobarbital and ethyl alcohol. The foregoing work, it is true, gives no direct evidence regarding the effect of the barbiturates on the lethal dose of alcohol, but when such marked synergism occurs with anesthetic doses it is the more surprising that Haggard and his coworkers (10) should have found the fatal dose of alcohol to be unaffected by large doses of amytal.

Oxygen.—There is ample supporting evidence for the finding that the administration of oxygen is ineffective in increasing the lethal dose of alcohol. Barach (38), although claiming some slight improvement in performance of alcoholic human subjects when in an atmosphere of oxygen, reported that a lethal dose of alcohol killed as many rabbits in an atmosphere containing 50 to 90% oxygen as in air, while Butler (39) found oxygen to have no effect on the mortality of mice intoxicated with alcohol.

Acid-base balance.—That the sensitivity of the cells of the central nervous system to alcohol may be altered by changes in the acid-base balance of the blood was demonstrated by Levy (40). She has found the minimal anesthetic dose for normal rats on rapid intravenous injection to average 2.16 mg. per gram. Rats made acidotic by the intravenous injection of 2.5% hydrochloric acid in a dose of 0.5 mg. per gram, however, required only 2.0 mg. per gram to produce anesthesia. Moreover, while the concentration of alcohol in the anesthetic normal rats averaged 388 mg.%, that of the equally depressed acidotic rats was but 330 mg.%, indicating that acidosis renders the brain cells of the rat hypersensitive to the anesthetic effects of alcohol. Whether or not the same would apply to the lethal effect remains to be shown.

Blood sugar.—Another factor influencing the lethal concentration of alcohol is the concentration of sugar in the blood. Thus Haggard and Greenberg (41), using the technic of divided intraperitoneal doses and analysis of jugular blood at respiratory failure already described, found that, while the lethal concentration in normal rats with a blood sugar concentration of 100 mg.% was 9.30 mg. per cubic centimeter, if the blood sugar was reduced to 70 mg.% by prolonged fasting, the lethal concentration was reduced to 8.0 mg. per cubic centimeter; and if the blood sugar was raised to 200 mg.% by forced feeding of sugar, the lethal concentration rose to 12.0 mg. per cubic centimeter. The intraperitoneal dosages required to produce death were 6.5 gm. per kilogram with blood sugar of 70 mg.%, 7.75 gm. with blood sugar of 100 mg.%, and 11.0 gm. per kilogram with blood sugar of 200 mg.%. The authors stated that, while these results were produced with grain alcohol, with other types of alcohol the lethal jugular concentration is the same but the dose required to produce this concentration varies, which they claim indicates a difference in the rate of oxidation of alcohol from various sources. It seems to us a much more likely explanation would be a difference in rate of absorption from the peritoneal cavity, which must be profoundly affected by even small amounts of substances other than alcohol in the mixtures. The conclusion of the authors that they have found a factor influencing the pharmacologic effects of alcohol should, we think, be modified, since they investigated but one effect, the paralysis of the respiratory center, and no evidence whatever is presented to support the implication that other effects of alcohol are influenced by blood sugar concentration.

Effect of alcohol in the psychoses and psychoneuroses.—Although it is a matter of common knowledge that individuals of different personality types respond in divergent ways to alcohol, there are very few controlled observations bearing on this point, which may be of considerable importance in the etiology of alcoholism. It has long been held that people who have sustained trauma to the head are subsequently more susceptible to alcohol; yet no objective evidence in support of this theory has been obtained. Indirect support for it is, however, derived from the experiments of Gantt (7), who found that while in normal dogs a dose of 0.5 cc. per kilogram of alcohol had no effect on cortical activity as judged by effect on conditioned reflexes, the same dose in an animal with half of the cerebral cortex removed produced a definite reduction of the reflex response. Thus it would seem that organic damage to the brain may be accompanied by increased susceptibility to alcohol.

Gantt was also of the opinion that the less emotionally stable of his dogs showed the most effect of alcohol in all the doses used. We are willing to grant his ability to separate the dogs into groups on the basis of emotional stability; as a matter of fact this may be fairly adequately accomplished by selection of breed alone. Whether, however, we can safely assume that the effect of alcohol as indicated by the conditioned reflex response will correlate well with, for example, the effect on neuromuscular co-ordination is not so clear; and further work directed along these lines is indicated.

In man, there have been a few observations on the general

behavior of the individual after administration of alcohol. The subjects have in all cases been suffering from psychoses or psychoneuroses, comparisons being made between them and "normals" rather than between normal subjects of different personality types. Perelman (42) gave 25 cc. of 50% alcohol by mouth to schizophrenics, repeating the dose once if necessary. He stated that all of the subjects "got drunk," although the dose is really quite small. There was crying and laughing, and contact with the examiner was improved.

Newman (43) compared the general reactions of groups of psychoneurotic and schizophrenic patients with a control series consisting of patients with organic disease of the nervous system without obvious psychiatric disease. That the control subjects could not strictly speaking be considered normal was recognized; however, they were more closely related to the experimental material in age and in economic and cultural status, as well as in their attitude as patients in a hospital situation, than would have been many more normal groups. It was emphasized that any investigation of the effects of alcohol presents an additional difficulty that is not present with agents that are not familiar to the subject or which can be easily and effectively disguised. Since the reaction of the inebriate is familiar to everyone, it is reasonable to expect that the reaction of an individual to alcohol would be a combination of the action of the drug itself and of the subject's interpretation of the action of alcohol based on his personal and vicarious experience. In an effort to eliminate this factor of suggestion, the alcohol was administered by the intravenous route—an expedient which was successful in the majority of cases, although a few experienced individuals were definitely suspicious of the identity of the material injected. The elimination of the factor of absorption, with the resultant variation in rate of increment and maximum concentration of alcohol in the blood, was also a desirable end accomplished by this route of administration. A uniform technic of administration was adhered to throughout the investigation. The solution employed consisted of 10% by volume of 95% alcohol in normal saline, prepared aseptically. The dose was calculated on body surface rather than body weight, as it was felt that this would result in a more uniform maximum blood alcohol concentration in the series. Each patient was given 40 cc. of 95% alcohol per square meter of body surface, equivalent roughly to 1.0 cc. per kilogram, the injection requiring one hour. The average maximum blood alcohol concentration attained was 112 mg.%, and the course of the blood alcohol curve paralleled quite closely that after ingestion of the same dose on an empty stomach.

Fifty subjects were included in the series. Of these, 9 patients with organic disease constituted the control group. They showed a rather constant reaction to alcohol, varying in a quantitative rather than a qualitative sense. All showed increased rapport with the physician, not, however, partaking of the extravagances of demonstration shown by certain of the psychoneurotic group. Three experienced an increased feeling of well-being, while none became sufficiently depressed to give way to tears. Increased loquacity was universally evident, the topics of conversation being general in nature. Slight dysarthria was occasionally present, and drowsiness was evident in some degree; but there was in no case evidence of loss of contact with reality, and aggressiveness and pugnacity were entirely absent.

There were 32 patients in the psychoneurotic group. No mention was made of the types of psychoneurotic reactions involved. The better rapport noted in the normal group was absent in a third of these subjects but when present was often very marked, the attachment being in some cases overtly sexual. Increased communicativeness was common, conversation hinging largely on symptomatology. A quarter of the subjects became moderately euphoric, while a slightly larger number cried. Increased suggestibility was very evident, hysterical seizures being easily induced in several cases.

There were 9 schizophrenics, 3 cases being of some duration, the remainder early. In contrast with the other two groups these patients showed no tendency to become increasingly friendly with the physician. One patient became more communicative; but in a number of cases increased loss of contact with reality resulted in an increase in verbal productivity concerned with delusional and hallucinatory experiences which could not rightly be considered as evidence of closer relationship with the patient. In no case was euphoria evident, while half the subjects cried, frequently with no other evidence of depression. In one case a catatonic state developed in a patient in whom the diagnosis had previously been undecided.

The difference in reaction of these hospital patients to alcohol, as contrasted with that seen, let us say, at a cocktail party where the concentration of alcohol in the blood would not be much different, may be explained by two facts: First, the environment in which the alcohol was given was not that usually associated with drinking; and, second, there was not the knowledge of having taken alcohol. In a majority of instances the alcohol was effective in breaking through the subject's reserve; but the change in affective tone was in general a quantitative rather than a qualitative one. Since most of the subjects were ill, and thus depressed or anxious, it is not remarkable that the incidence of tears was greater by far than one would expect in social drinking. In spite of the smallness of the series, certain tendencies to difference in reaction to alcohol by the various reaction types were evident. In contrast to the increased volubility, improved rapport, and exaggeration of symptoms on the part of the psychoneurotic were the antagonism, increased dissociation, and elaboration of delusional content in schizophrenics. The possibility of making use of alcohol in the differential diagnosis of these conditions was pointed out.

Kantarovich and Constantinovich (25) administered alcohol to 15 patients with catatonic manifestations. At first brandy containing 40% alcohol was given by mouth, in dosage equivalent to 1 to 2 gm. alcohol per kilogram. Fifteen cubic centimeters of the brandy were given at intervals of from 3 to 6 minutes; but because of lack of co-operation of the subjects it was found necessary to change to the intravenous route, 100 to 500 cc. of a 20% solution of alcohol in water being given in 20 to 60 minutes, the injection being stopped when drowsiness supervened. In 11 of the 15 subjects there was a disappearance of mutism, 4 of these maintaining their improvement for a considerable time. In the remaining 4 patients the alcohol produced no effect. The authors felt that their results were not in accord with those of Newman (43), in that they found an increased verbal productivity in a large majority of cases. However, perusal of their protocols reveals that the increased productivity consisted exclusively of elaboration of delusional and hallucinatory material, which, although it might well be considered an improvement in a mute patient, nevertheless is quite in accord with the finding by Newman of increased loss of contact with reality and uncovering of delusional trends not evident without alcohol. Thus the two observations are not contradictory but rather supplement each other in covering together a broader range of the manifestations of schizophrenia. The authors felt that the procedure, in addition to being of some value in discovering the psychotic trend in mute patients, might be of therapeutic value as well, on the basis of the four patients who showed continued improvement after it.

Thorner (44) reported that the effect of the intravenous injection of 6 to 9 grains of sodium amytal in 4 to 5 minutes produced the same effect as alcohol, although no data on the effect of the latter drug appears in his contribution. In fact, he found a disappearance of catatonic phenomena, improved rapport with the examiner, and less evidence of delusions. These observations of the effect of amytal are in accord with many others. This effect is, however, quite unlike the effect of alcohol in schizophrenia in our experience. In a number of cases we have (45) administered alcohol and amytal to the same schizophrenic patient on different occasions, both by the intravenous route and in dosage adequate to produce drowsiness or sleep. The reaction to the two depressant agents has been quite in contrast, alcohol generally producing an intensification of the schizophrenic reaction, while amytal not infrequently has produced a complete remission—fleeting to be sure, but consisting of a qualitative rather than a quantitative change in behavior. Further investigation of the action of these two agents in schizophrenia is needed, particularly when we consider that their seat of action is considered to be different, alcohol acting primarily on the cortex and amytal on the thalamus and basal ganglia. The possible connotation as to the localization of aberrance of function in schizophrenia is obvious.

Trapp and Schube (61) administered alcohol to a group of 21 psychotic subjects, of whom 13 were males and 8 females. There were 15 cases of dementia precox, of which 1 was a simple schizophrenic, 1 was a hebephrenic, 9 were catatonic, and 4 were paranoid. There were also 3 psychoses with mental deficiency and 3 manic depressives in the depressed phase. The duration of the psychosis varied from 6 months to 13 years. The alcohol was given as a 40% solution in water by nasal tube, a little at a time, the total dose being 180 cc. of this solution, or approximately 1.0 cc. per kilogram of alcohol. In 8 cases the alcohol was given again on another day. All 9 of the catatonic schizophrenics had been mute for more than 6 months; of these 5 talked in varying degree with alcohol. Of the 4 paranoid schizophrenics 3 were mutes, and of these 2 talked with alcohol. The two mute mental defectives and the one mute depressed patient all talked with alcohol. The emotional state of the simple schizophrenic was unchanged, that of the hebephrenic was enhanced. Of the 4 paranoids, 2 were unchanged and 1 became belligerent. Of the 9 catatonics, 5 displayed sorrow, alternating in 3 with silly laughter, while 3 were indifferent and 1 became frankly erotic. Negativism, which was present in 6 of the schizophrenics, did not change. The authors claim temporary therapeutic benefit of the injection in 6 cases, which persisted over a month in but one. The authors considered the diminution in mutism not to be in accord with Newman's findings. It must be remembered, however, that the material dealt with was quite different, Newman's cases being in the incipiency of their psychosis. If one examines the protocols, which are quite complete, one cannot but be struck by the similarity of the responses to those of Newman's patients, with the very evident fact that, although mutism might disappear and an elaboration of delusions and hallucinations occur, the change was always quantitative rather than qualitative in nature and consisted of an intensification of the underlying behavior pattern. The authors felt that the procedure might possibly have some therapeutic value, as well as be occasionally useful in establishing a diagnosis, although they were of the opinion that the differential diagnosis of mental deficiency and simple schizophrenia was not made easier by this expedient. The value of the procedure in determining the delusional content in mute patients was perhaps its most important asset.

In summary, it seems that the effect of alcohol is to intensify the existing mood, effecting a quantitative rather than a qualitative change, and making manifest abnormalities of behavior which might otherwise have escaped notice. This is in keeping with the drinking habits of individuals: the social drinker most frequently uses alcohol relatively in moderation to intensify his pleasure, while the despondent solitary drinker seeks anesthesia from very large doses, receiving no consolation from the drug until this stage of its action is reached. In fact, not infrequently the increase in depression experienced before anesthetic doses are achieved is such as to result in suicidal attempts, a possible explanation for the very considerable incidence of suicidal attempts among alcoholics.

Effect on personality.—We have seen that individuals suffering from psychiatric disease usually developing in definitely divergent personality types react quite differently to alcohol. No work has been done on individuals within the normal range of personality variation; but it is reasonable to assume that they also might be expected to be differently affected by alcohol according to their makeup, just as was the case with Gantt's dogs. So far we have referred to the changes in general behavior, mood, and emotional stability, all factors difficult of appraisal but nevertheless of importance, particularly from the medicolegal aspect; for it is just such changes which, equally with interference with neuromuscular co-ordination, are responsible for bringing the individual into conflict with the law. As a matter of fact, in respect to most crimes in which alcohol plays a part it is entirely the change in personality which is responsible, the depression of co-ordination frequently being the factor which limits the seriousness of the act by interfering with its execution. Motor co-ordination, however, lends itself much more to scientific investigation; and since it also must be conceded to play an important part in the effect of alcohol on such skilled acts as driving a motor car, it is natural that in this particular connection stress has been laid on this aspect almost to the exclusion of the effect on personality. Nor is there any very good evidence to show whether or not there is any degree of parallelism between the effect of alcohol on the personality and that on neuromuscular co-ordination; and it is only when objective tests have shown that certain individuals do not show significant changes in coordination at blood alcohol values generally shown to produce a greatly increased hazard in driving a car that these other effects of alcohol are invoked to explain the discrepancy, in spite of the fact that they have been studied little if at all. Such studies, on a quantitative, scientific basis, are a necessary complement to already initiated studies of the effect of alcohol on neuromuscular co-ordination if we are to have any rational basis for the chemical diagnosis of drunkenness. We shall deal with this subject in detail later; let us now consider the evidence at hand bearing on individual tolerance to alcohol, inherent and acquired, keeping in mind that the data embrace but one aspect of the problem—the effect on neuromuscular co-ordination.

Variability in effect.—We should not be surprised to find that different individuals are affected in different degree by the same concentration of alcohol in their brains when we consider the universality of variability in response to drugs indicated by Nelson (46), which extends to even such definite events as lethal doses, as for instance the variation of 2½ to 1 for the fatal dose of digitalis in the cat. The importance of this variability is in connection with the validity of the setting up of certain definite concentrations of alcohol in the blood as absolute evidence of intoxication, and it is because of this very practical application that we belabor the point.

Inherent tolerance to alcohol.—This variation in inherent tolerance to alcohol is apparent in all the well-documented attempts to correlate the alcohol content of body fluids with drunkenness, although it is often neglected in a discussion of the results in favor of emphasis on the undeniable correlation which exists in a majority of instances between alcohol concentration and inebriation. Bogen (47) tested 300 patients brought to the Cincinnati General Hospital on suspicion of drunkenness, determining breath or urine alcohol concentrations and examining the patients clinically. A clinical diagnosis of drunkenness was made only in the presence of unmistakable loss of control of speech and movement. No patient with less than 1.0 mg. alcohol per cubic centimeter was adjudged intoxicated, while half of those with 1.0 to 2.0 mg., three-fourths of those with 3.0 mg., and *almost* every patient with 4.0 mg. or above were found to be drunk. Thus while a considerable number of subjects were considered drunk at a concentration of 1.0 to 2.0 mg. per cubic centimeter, some few were not so considered at concentrations twice this great.

Jetter (24) examined 1,000 cases, a group similar to that of Bogen. Gross tests of inco-ordination were used in the clinical diagnosis to make the study as objective as possible. It was found that while 10.5% were diagnosed as drunk with blood alcohol concentration of 50 mg.%, 6.7% of the group with blood alcohols of 400 mg.% were adjudged sober. To quote this author: "when it is realized that at 0.40% alcohol, a concentration close to the lethal point, that an individual may show so little effects as to be adjudged sober by our criteria, or on the other hand may be in coma at this same level, it becomes evident that there exists a marked variation in the individual's reaction to alcohol." Nor did this author change his opinion that individual tolerance to alcohol was a potent factor after study (48) of an additional 800 patients.

Bahnsen and Vedel-Petersen (3), studying the effect of the administration of alcohol on tests of neuromuscular co-ordination, were impressed with the variation in degree from subject to subject. This variation was noted by Turner (49) in an experimental study of the relation of blood alcohol to intoxication in the dog. He administered alcohol by stomach tube, and took samples of heart's blood at 30 minutes and 1, 2, 3, 4, 5, and 6 hours thereafter. The degrees of drunkenness were designated *N* for normal, *M* for loss of memory, *E* for loss of equilibrium, *EM* for loss of both memory and equilibrium. Blood alcohol concentrations and degrees of drunkenness were plotted in the case of 2 dogs, one of which received 2 gm. of alcohol per kilogram and the other 3 gm. The first dog showed loss of memory and equilibrium at a blood alcohol concentration of 285 mg.%, while the second showed perfectly normal behavior.

Newman and Card (50, 51) and Newman and Lehman (52), working with dogs in a study of tolerance acquired on habituation to alcohol, found definite evidence of variation in the degree of drunkenness at a given level of blood alcohol concentration. This difference in tolerance within the group was present both when abstinent and when habituated. The range of blood alcohol concentrations at which all animals showed the same degree of inebriation amounted to as much as 75 to 100 mg.%, and was about equal to the increase in tolerance brought about by habituation.

Effect of other factors on inherent tolerance.—It should be unnecessary to do more than note in passing that other factors tending to reduce neuromuscular control, such as shock, drugs, carbon monoxide, low-oxygen tension, and so on, may be additive to the effects of alcohol, so that an individual having to cope with one or more of these as well may show much more evidence of drunkenness at the same blood alcohol concentration than he would under more favorable circumstances. That changes in the blood metabolites, notably blood sugar concentration, may also play a part in determining tolerance to alcohol at any particular time is indicated by the work of Haggard and Greenberg (41), who found the fatal dose of alcohol to vary directly with the blood sugar concentration, an increase in the blood sugar of the rat from 70 to 200 mg.% increasing the fatal dose from 6.5 to 11.0 gm. per kilogram. Should this effect also apply to the sublethal intoxicating doses, it might be expected to result in an individual tolerance to alcohol varying considerably from hour to hour, depending on the blood sugar level, which varies in relation to meals and exercise. Further work on this point is needed, and the technic used by Turner and by Newman and his coworkers noted above should be applicable to the problem.

Tolerance acquired by habituation.—Considerable as is the variation in inherent tolerance to alcohol, to this we must add that brought about by habituation to alcohol over a long period. That such a tolerance exists has been amply demonstrated, and in previous chapters we have presented evidence indicating with reasonable certainty that it is not due to decreased absorption, increased elimination, or increased rate of metabolism of alcohol, but rather is a tissue tolerance, the habituated organism showing less evidence of intoxication at the same blood and brain alcohol concentration after habituation than before. We need not, then, concern ourselves here with the volume of work directed at the mechanism of tolerance to alcohol but may rather outline the data available regarding its extent.

Although the fact of the existence of acquired tolerance to alcohol is denied by no one, a number of investigators have stated that the tolerance is to the amount of alcohol consumed and not to the concentration in the blood or brain. Bogen (53) in 1936 reviewed the literature, and was unable to come to any definite conclusion. He had been unable to produce by habituation a strain of fruit flies resistant to alcohol. He denied the existence of tissue tolerance to alcohol, seemingly on the basis of his undoubtedly correct statement that with a concentration below 10 mg.% no test will reveal any degree of alcoholic intoxication, below 100 mg.% no one is clinically drunk (Jetter [24] would disagree), and no one can withstand 1,000 mg.% and live. Even if we are not inclined to quarrel with these limits, however, there is plenty of latitude for exhibition of a very considerable difference in tolerance from one individual to another. Gettler and Tiber (54), on the basis of analysis of the brains of individuals coming to autopsy, stated that the effect of alcohol was irrespective of the alcoholic habits of the individual; and Gettler (22) stated: "If there is 0.25% in the brain, the man becomes unbalanced, whether an habituee or not." He noted the difficulty of securing adequate evidence of presence or absence of intoxication in autopsy material. Jetter (55) gave alcohol in doses up to 2 cc. per kilogram by mouth to 20 normal young adults, and judged their drunkenness by the same criteria which he used in his much larger series of hospital patients. In the experimental series, consisting of abstainers or occasional drinkers, he found an incidence of drunkenness of 50% at 100 mg.%, 57% at 150 mg.%, and 100% at 200 mg.%, as contrasted with 18.5%, 47.0%, and 83.6% at these concentrations in the hospital patients, who were presumably habituated. The lower incidence of drunkenness at the same blood alcohol concentration in the hospital patients he attributed possibly to their habituation. Several other possible explanations exist, however. The greater degree of intoxication while the blood alcohol concentration is ascending has been noted. This situation prevailed in the experimental subjects, presumably not in the hospital subjects. Also, during the absorptive period it has been shown that arterial blood alcohol is much higher than systemic venous blood alcohol, and brain alcohol concentration is more closely related to arterial than to venous blood alcohol. Since the hospital patients were probably in the post-absorptive phase, when the two concentrations are approximately equal, venous blood alcohol concentration reflected accurately brain alcohol concentration, while with the experimental subjects, in the absorptive phase, arterial and brain alcohol concentrations were undoubtedly higher than the values found in the venous blood, accounting for the greater degree of drunkenness noted. Even should these considerations invalidate this evidence of the existence of acquired tolerance, a further possibility must be borne in mind. That is that the presumably habituated individuals brought to the hospital for suspected alcoholism may well be suspected of having an inherently low tolerance for alcohol to account for their apprehension, with the result that we should not expect even a period of habituation to give them a tolerance equal to that of a more general cross-section of non-habituated individuals. All of this discussion is of necessity more philosophical than objective and scientific, and we must turn to animal experimentation for more accurate observations on acquired tolerance.

Turner (49) habituated one dog to alcohol by giving it 1.10 gm. of alcohol per kilogram daily for 18 days After an interval of 48 hours, a test dose of 3 gm. per kilogram was given, and the blood alcohol concentration and the degree of inebriation were followed for 6 hours. Unfortunately the alcohol tolerance of this dog was not tested before habituation; so we can only compare his performance with that of the small series of unhabituated dogs given similar test doses. On such comparison there seems to be little difference in the degree of drunkenness exhibited by the habituated dog and the controls at the same blood alcohol level; but such is the degree of variation between the control animals that a considerable tolerance incidental to habituation may well have been obscured. Also, the dosage and period of habituation are not as great as might be desired.

Levy (56, 57, 58) habituated a group of white rats by daily injections of alcohol, gradually working up to doses of 2.5 cc. of 60% alcohol per rat per day. The period of habituation varied from 3 to 6 months. At the end of the period of habituation she determined the dose of alcohol injected intravenously in one minute which would produce a period of anesthesia (as judged by response to pinching a muscle with a Kocher clamp) of 3 minutes. This was found to be 28% greater in the habituated rats than in a large series of controls. The minimal lethal dose, administered under the same conditions, was found to be 10% higher in the habituated animals, indicating that the tolerance for moderate concentrations exceeded that for higher ones. Analyses of the blood and brain alcohol concentrations of habituated and control animals sacrificed at intervals after injection showed no difference between the two groups given the same dose; but the brain alcohol concentration of the habituated animals was distinctly higher at the same degree of anesthesia than that of the abstainers, indicating beyond a doubt the existence of an acquired tissue tolerance to alcohol.

Newman and Card (50) habituated a group of three dogs by placing them on a fluid intake consisting solely of a solution of alcohol in water of gradually increasing concentration, so that at the end of 3 months they were drinking 10% alcohol, on which they were maintained for 10 months. Over this period they received on an average 6.8 cc. of alcohol per kilogram body weight, an amount equal to a quart of 90-proof whisky for a 70 kg. man. At the end of the total of 13 months of habituation, these three dogs and another group of three which had never had alcohol were given a dose of 4.0 cc. per kilogram intravenously at a rate of 0.5 cc. of 20% alcohol per kilogram per minute, and the blood alcohol concentration and the degree of drunkenness were followed at frequent intervals over a period of 7 hours. Nine stages of intoxication in the dog were delineated, the most severe being anesthesia as evidenced by abolition of the corneal reflex, and the least severe consisting of the slightest discernible ataxia on climbing a short flight of stairs. It was found that these states could be judged with a fair degree of uniformity by different observers. They are enumerated below:

SCALE OF DEGREES OF DRUNKENNESS IN THE DOG

1. Not ataxic on the level, slight ataxia on stairs
2. Not ataxic on the level, moderately ataxic on stairs
3. Slightly ataxic on the level, cannot climb stairs
4. Grossly ataxic but able to walk briskly
5. Able to stand and walk 1 or 2 steps
6. Cannot stand but attempts voluntary movements
7. Responds to stimuli only by blinking; lets head fall slowly to floor when it is dropped
8. No response to stimuli; lets head flop on floor when it is dropped; corneal reflex present
9. Corneal reflex absent

Curves of blood alcohol concentration for the two groups were practically coincidental. The degree of drunkenness was, however, definitely less for the habituated animals than for the normal controls. This tolerance was most marked with moderate concentrations of alcohol, being absent with anesthetic concentrations. This was in accord with the finding that the minimal anesthetic dose, as judged by abolition of the corneal reflex with slow intravenous administration of alcohol, was not significantly different in the two groups. Although this is not entirely in accord with the findings of Levy (56, 57, 58), who demonstrated a tolerance to anesthetic concentrations in the rat, it must be remembered that she also found less tolerance to higher concentrations, and also that the rate of administration in her case was extremely rapid, so that changes in rate of alcohol distribution may have played a complicating part.

When the same test dose of 4.0 cc. per kilogram was given to the animals of Newman and Card by stomach tube, a rather different picture was evident. As we have already described, the blood alcohol concentration rose higher and more rapidly in the habituated animals than in the abstainers, with the result that during the first two hours these animals were definitely more intoxicated than were the abstainers, owing to their considerably higher blood alcohol concentration. After this period, however, the blood alcohol concentrations of the two groups coming closer together, the habituated animals again manifested their increased tolerance. This experiment indicates the futility of experiments in which a comparison is made of the behavior of habituated and nonhabituated individuals after a given dose of alcohol by mouth, since here the difference in rate of absorption was sufficient not only to obscure but to reverse the evidence of tolerance, which was made apparent only by the curves of blood alcohol concentration.

Unfortunately Newman and Card had not conceived the idea of correlating behavior and blood alcohol concentration until after the three dogs had been habituated to alcohol, so that they had to be compared with other animals as controls, with the attendant possibility of differences in inherent tolerance obscuring the issue. To circumvent this difficulty, and to determine also if acquired tolerance to alcohol were a temporary or permanent phenomenon, the same group of dogs was kept without alcohol for seven months (51), at the end of which time the intravenous test dose was again administered and blood alcohol and behavior were followed for seven hours. It was at once apparent that tolerance had been lost, the average curve of blood alcohol against degree of drunkenness corresponding very closely with that of the group of control dogs used in the previous experiment. Individual differences in tolerance were again very apparent, the curve of the least tolerant dog when habituated coinciding with that of the most tolerant dog after abstinence—further evidence of the necessity of comparing behavior in the same animal before and after habituation, unless a large series of animals is used.

In order to fulfill this criterion and to substantiate the previous work, Newman and Lehman (52) followed the blood alcohol concentration and the behavior of a new series of five dogs, and subsequently habituated them to alcohol by allowing them to drink as much as they wanted of 10% alcohol in water for two-hour periods night and morning, no fluid being allowed them at other times. Under these circumstances they had to drink large quantities in a short period of time and became quite drunk twice daily, a phenomenon which did not occur when the previous series was allowed access to the alcohol at all times and were able to drink a little at a time. Thus the conditions of the experiment more nearly fulfilled those of human chronic alcoholism. The animals consumed 6.9 cc. of alcohol per kilogram daily, approximately the same as did the preceding series. The test dose was given intravenously in the same manner as in the other experiment. At the end of three months of habituation, the test was given again. Plotting the degrees of drunkenness against blood alcohol concentration, a clear-cut difference between the averages of the two tests, before and after habituation, was apparent, there being this time actually no overlap between the groups. From this evidence there cannot be the slightest doubt that at least in the dog a tissue tolerance to alcohol may be developed by habituation.

Tolerance of alcoholics to other agents.—Since it has long been held by anesthetists that alcoholics are resistant to ether anesthesia, Abreu and Emerson (59) investigated this phenomenon in animals. They used mice, and determined the time required for induction of anesthesia as judged by loss of the righting reflex when the animals were placed in a concentration of ether of 2.2 millimols per liter. They then gave daily intraperitoneal injections of alcohol for 7 weeks, starting at a dose of 2.0 cc. per kilogram and going up to 12.0 cc. per kilogram twice daily the last week. Controls were treated with saline injections, and the induction time was tested weekly, a period of 24 hours without alcohol preceding the test. During the first 3 weeks on alcohol, the induction time showed a considerable increase in length; but by the fifth week it was the same as in the controls, and subsequently became even shorter. The authors are unable to explain this observation; but a possibility remains that with the larger doses the 24-hour period of abstinence before the test of etherization was not sufficient to remove all the alcohol, with the result that a certain amount of depression from alcohol was already present and the induction time was thus shortened.

Ahlquist and Dille (60) tested the reactions of alcohol tolerant rabbits to a variety of agents. A test dose of alcohol of 1.5 gm. per kilogram was given intravenously as a 10% solution at the rate of 10 cc. per minute, and the "sleeping time" as judged by the period during which the righting reflex was lost was noted. Habituation was then carried out by intraperitoneal injection of 1.5 gm. per kilogram daily as a 20% solution for from 15 to 25 days. After an abstinent period of 48 hours to insure elimination of all the alcohol, the intravenous test dose was again administered and the sleeping time was found to be reduced by half, confirming the existence of acquired tolerance already demonstrated by other workers in rats and dogs. An abstinent period of but six days was, however, sufficient to cause the disappearance of the tolerance. The tolerant rabbits were found to be resistant to pentobarbital and to evipal, while it required 1.28 cc. of ether per kilogram to induce anesthesia in them as contrasted with .87 cc. in nonhabituated animals. There was, however, no tolerance to the analgetic action of amidopyrine or the convulsant action of metrazol. The authors concluded that there exists a cross-tolerance of alcohol to other depressants of the central nervous system. It is interesting to speculate on whether the reverse is true and if subjects resistant to the barbiturates are resistant also to alcohol.

REFERENCES

1. Masserman, J. H., and Jacobson, L., "Effects of Ethyl Alcohol on the Cortex and Hypothalamus of the Cat," *Arch. Neurol. Psychiatry*, **43**:334, 1940

2. MASSERMAN, J. H., "Stimulant Effects of Ethyl Alcohol on Cortico-Hypothalamic Functions," *J. Pharmacol.*, **70**:450, 1940
3. BAHNSEN, P., and VEDEL-PETERSEN, K., "Alcohol Studies. I. Experiments on Drivers of Motor Vehicles," *J. Ind. Hyg.*, **16**:304, 1934
4. NEWMAN, H. W., and FLETCHER, E., "The Effect of Alcohol on Driving Skill," *J. Am. Med. Assoc.*, **115**:1600, 1940
5. BERNHARD, C. G., and GOLDBERG, L., "Nystagmus spontané par suite d'intoxication aigue par l'alcool," *Acta Med. Scand.*, **84**:36, 1934
6. AVDEYEV, L. A., "The Effect of Single and Repeated Doses of Alcohol on Conditioned Reflexes in the Dog," *Arch. intern. pharmacodynamie*, **48**:117, 1934
7. GANTT, W. H., "Effect of Alcohol on Cortical and Subcortical Activity Measured by the Conditioned Reflex Method," *Bull. Johns Hopkins Hosp.*, **56**:61, 1935
8. MULLIN, F. J., KLEITMAN, N., and COOPERMAN, N. R., "Studies on the Physiology of Sleep. X. The Effect of Alcohol and Caffeine on Motility and Body Temperature during Sleep," *Am. J. Physiol.*, **106**:478, 1934
9. MCFARLAND, R. A., and BARACH, A. L., "The Relationship between Alcoholic Intoxication and Anoxemia," *Am. J. Med. Sci.*, **192**:186, 1936
10. HAGGARD, H. W., GREENBERG, L. A., RAKIETEN, N., and COHEN, L. H., "Studies on the Absorption, Distribution, and Elimination of Alcohol. VII," *J. Pharmacol.*, **69**:266, 1940
11. GOLDFARB, W., and WORTIS, J., "The Availability of Ethyl Alcohol for Human Brain Oxidations," *Quart. J. Stud. Alcohol*, **1**:268, 1940
12. WORTIS, J., BOWMAN, K. M., and GOLDFARB, W., "Human Brain Metabolism," *Am. J. Psychiatry*, **97**:552, 1940
13. GOLDFARB, W., BOWMAN, K. M., and WORTIS, J., "The Effect of Alcohol on Cerebral Metabolism," *Am. J. Psychiatry*, **97**:384, 1940
14. WORTIS, S. B., "Respiratory Metabolism of Excised Brain Tissue. II. The Effects of Some Drugs on Brain Oxidations," *Arch. Neurol. Psychiatry*, **33**:1022, 1935
15. COLSON, Z. W., "The Effect of Alcohol on Vision: an Experimental Investigation," *J. Am. Med. Assoc.*, **115**:1525, 1940
16. NEWMAN, H. W., and FLETCHER, E., unpublished data
17. PETT, L. B., "Mobilization of Vitamin A by Alcohol," *Science*, **92**:63, 1940
18. CLAUSTEN, S. W., BAUM, W. S., MCCOORD, A. B., RYDEEN, J. O., and BREESE, B. B., "Mobilization of Vitamin A from Its Stores in the Tissues," *Science*, **91**:318, 1940
19. CLAUSTEN, S. W., BREESE, B. B., BAUM, W. S., MCCOORD, A. B., and RYDEEN, J. O., "Effect of Alcohol on Vitamin A Content of Blood in Human Subjects," *Science*, **93**:21, 1940
20. MUEHLBERGER, C. W., "Relative Toxicological Effects of Synthetic Ethanol and Grain Fermentation Ethanol in Blended Whiskies," *Am. J. Pub. Health*, **25**:1132, 1935
21. BARLOW, O. W., "Studies on the Pharmacology of Ethyl Alcohol," *J. Pharmacol.*, **56**:117, 1936

22. GETTLER, A. O., "Chemical Evidences of Alcoholic Intoxication and Their Medicolegal Significance," *New Engl. J. Med.*, **201**:725, 1929
23. GETTLER, A. O., and FREIREICH, A. W., "Determination of Alcoholic Intoxication during Life by Spinal Fluid Analysis," *J. Biol. Chem.*, **92**:199, 1931
24. JETTER, W. W., "Studies in Alcohol. I. The Diagnosis of Acute Intoxication by a Correlation of Clinical and Chemical Findings," *Am. J. Med. Sci.*, **196**:475, 1938
25. KANTAROVICH, N. V., and CONSTANTINOVICH, S. K., "The Effect of Alcohol in Catatonic Syndromes," *Am. J. Psychiatry*, **96**:651, 1935
26. MEHRTENS, H. G., and NEWMAN, H. W., "Alcohol Injected Intravenously: Its Penetration into the Cerebrospinal Fluid in Man," *Arch. Neurol. Psychiatry*, **30**:1092, 1933
27. NEWMAN, H. W., and MEHRTENS, H. G., "Effect of Intravenous Injection of Ethyl Alcohol on Gastric Secretion in Man," *Proc. Soc. Exper. Biol. and Med.*, **30**:145, 1932
28. MUNCH, J. C., and SCHWARTZ, E. W., "Narcotic and Toxic Potency of Aliphatic Alcohols upon Rabbits," *J. Lab. Clin. Med.*, **10**:985, 1925
29. LEHMAN, A. J., and NEWMAN, H. W., "Comparative Intravenous Toxicity of Some Monohydric Saturated Alcohols," *J. Pharmacol.*, **61**:103, 1937
30. HAGGARD, H. W., GREENBERG, L. A., and RAKIETEN, N., "Studies on the Absorption, Distribution, and Elimination of Alcohol. VI," *J. Pharmacol.*, **69**:252, 1940
31. NEWMAN, H. W., unpublished data
32. MELLANBY, E., *Alcohol: Its Absorption into and Disappearance from the Blood under Different Conditions*, National Research Council (Great Britain) Special Report Series, No. 31, 1919
33. GOLD, H., and TRAVELL, J., "Strychnine in Poisoning by Alcohol," *J. Pharmacol.*, **52**:345, 1932
34. CARRIERE, G., HURIEZ, C., and WILLOQUET, P., "Étude experimentale des injections intraveineuses d'alcool au cours d'intoxications par le gardenal," *Compt. rend. soc. biol.*, **116**:188, 1934
35. OLSZYCKA, L., "Étude quantitative des phénomènes de synergie. Potentialisation de l'action hypnotique chez la souris," *Compt. rend. acad. sci.*, **201**:796, 1935
36. OLSZYCKA, L., "Étude quantitative des phénomènes de synergie. Contribution à l'étude du mécanisme des phénomènes de potentialisation de l'action hypnotique chez le rat," *Compt. rend. acad. sci.*, **202**:1107, 1936
37. DILLE, J. L., and AHLQUIST, R. R., "The Synergism of Ethyl Alcohol and Sodium Pentobarbital," *J. Pharmacol.*, **61**:385, 1937
38. BARACH, A. L., "Action of Oxygen in Counteracting Intoxication," *Am. J. Physiol.*, **107**:610, 1934
39. BUTLER, T. C., "The Effect of Oxygen Inhalation on the Course of Alcoholic Intoxication," *J. Pharmacol.*, **58**:68, 1936
40. LEVY, J., "Alcoolisme expérimentale. Hypersensibilité cellulaire due à l'acidose," *Compt. rend. acad. sci.*, **200**:1069, 1935

41. Haggard, H. W., and Greenberg, L. A., "The Effects of Alcohol as Influenced by Blood Sugar," *Science*, **85**:608, 1937
42. Perelman, A. A., "Light Alcoholic Intoxication in Schizophrenia," *Rev. Psychiat. Neurol. and Reflexol.*, **5**:36, 1930
43. Newman, H. W., "Alcohol Injected Intravenously: Some Psychological and Psychopathological Effects in Man," *Am. J. Psychiatry*, **91**:1345, 1935
44. Thorner, M. W., "The Psychopharmacology of Sodium Amytal," *J. Nerv. and Ment. Dis.*, **81**:164, 1935
45. Newman, H. W., unpublished data
46. Nelson, E. E., "Variability in Response to Drugs," *J. Am. Med. Assoc.*, **113**:1373, 1939
47. Bogen, E., "Drunkenness: a Quantitative Study of Acute Alcoholic Intoxication," *J. Am. Med. Assoc.*, **89**:1508, 1927
48. Jetter, W. W., "Chemical and Clinical Diagnosis of Acute Alcoholism," *New Engl. J. Med.*, **221**:1019, 1939
49. Turner, R. G., "Blood Alcohol and Its Relation to Intoxication," *J. Pharmacol.*, **44**:305, 1932
50. Newman, H. W., and Card, J., "The Nature of Tolerance to Ethyl Alcohol," *J. Nerv. and Ment. Dis.*, **86**:428, 1937
51. Newman, H. W., and Card, J., "Duration of Acquired Tolerance to Ethyl Alcohol," *J. Pharmacol.*, **59**:249, 1937
52. Newman, H. W., and Lehman, A. J., "Nature of Acquired Tolerance to Alcohol," *J. Pharmacol.*, **62**:301, 1938
53. Bogen, E., "Tolerance to Alcohol: Its Mechanism and Significance," *Calif. and Western Med.*, **44**:262, 1936
54. Gettler, A. O., and Tiber, A., "The Alcoholic Content of the Human Brain: Its Relation to Intoxication," *Arch. Path. Lab. Med.*, **3**:218, 1927
55. Jetter, W. W., "Studies in Alcohol. II. Experimental Feeding of Alcohol to Nonalcoholic Individuals," *Am. J. Med. Sci.*, **196**:487, 1938
56. Levy, J., "Contribution à l'étude de l'accoutumance expérimentale aux poisons. I. Alcoolisme expérimentale," *Bull. soc. chim. biol.*, **17**:13, 1935
57. Levy, J., *ibid.* "II. Alcoolisme expérimentale, fixation de l'alcool sur les tissus de l'organisme accoutumé à cette substance," *Bull. soc. chim. biol.*, **17**:27, 1935
58. Levy, J., *ibid.* "III. Alcoolisme expérimentale. L'accoutumance à l'alcool peut-elle être considerée comme une conséquence de l'hyposensibilité cellulaire?" *Bull. soc. chim. biol.*, **17**:47, 1935
59. Abreu, B. E., and Emerson, G. A., "Susceptibility to Ether Anesthesia of Mice Habituated to Alcohol, Morphine, and Cocaine," *Anesthesia and Analgesia*, **18**:294, 1939
60. Ahlquist, R. P., and Dille, J. M., "Reactions of Alcohol Tolerant Rabbits to Pentobarbital, Evipal, Ether, Amidopyrine, and Metrazol," *J. Pharmacol.*, **70**:301, 1940
61. Trapp, C. E., and Schube, P. G., "The Reaction of Certain Psychotic Types to Alcohol," *J. Nerv. and Ment. Dis.*, **85**:668, 1937

CHAPTER V

THE CHEMICAL DIAGNOSIS OF DRUNKENNESS

A large proportion of the research in alcohol during the past decade or so has been inspired in some degree by the increasing importance of the diagnosis of inebriation. Before the advent of popular use of the automobile, the hazards of drunkenness were largely confined to the inebriate and possibly his immediate family. So long as a drunkard confined his activities to falling in stupor in the gutter, or throwing his boots at his wife's head when he returned home, he did not present an important threat to the public safety; and what efforts were made to curb his course were most often in the direction of saving his soul.

Now, however, when there is a fair probability that at some time during his debauch a heavy drinker will find himself in control of a motor vehicle, with all its potentialities as a lethal weapon, the situation takes on quite a different aspect; and, little as we may be concerned with the final repository of his soul, we have a very genuine concern for his activities at the wheel. He presents a menace on the highway in the face of which no amount of precaution, superior equipment, or skill on the part of sober users of the roads may be of any avail, with the result that when he comes to grief the innocent must suffer with the guilty. Nor is he dangerous only when driving; as a pedestrian he also presents a serious problem by his presence on the road—not so much for his own safety, which one might be inclined not to value too highly, but because motorists in seeking to avoid striking him may precipitate themselves into other vehicles.

For these reasons it is essential that the attitude of society and its agency of enforcement, the law, be informed regarding the offense variously entitled drunkenness, intoxication, and being under the influence of intoxicating liquor. However one may feel about society's responsibility for an individual's moral conduct, there can be no question about the necessity for safeguarding the lives and property of those with whom he comes in contact, even though it may entail certain restrictions of his activity. There thus arises the concept that a degree of alcoholic intoxication which need not cause an offense against society when the inebriate is in his own home may present a definite hazard to the public weal when he is on the public highway, either as the driver of a motor vehicle or as a pedestrian. The removal of such an individual from a position in which he endangers himself and others cannot be considered an infringement of personal liberty but must be regarded as a deprivation for cause of certain special privileges.

Definition of intoxication.—It is obviously necessary that some workable definition of the rather loose terms denoting the degree of inebriation which renders a man unsafe on a public road must be incorporated in the law before any uniform administration of justice in this regard can take place. The Committee on Tests for Intoxication of the Street and Highway Traffic Section of the National Safety Council in their *Progress Report* for 1937 (1) presented the information relative to the definition of the terms "intoxicated" and "under the influence of intoxicating liquor" as provided at their request by the attorneys general of the various states. These definitions varied widely from state to state, but they can to some extent be placed in a relatively few categories. Thus in no less than 24 states at this time there was no legal definition of either term, the understanding of such matters being considered common knowledge and thus for decision by the jury. The other 24 states fell roughly into three groups: The first group we will consider consisted of 12 states, in which the definition of either or both of the terms corresponded essentially with the Arizona definition of "under the influence." In several of these states there were separate interpretations of the two terms, the more serious degree of affection being reserved for the term "intoxicated," but the less serious degree, "under the influence," being the offense so far as operating motor vehicles was concerned. This seems a desirable situation, since it permits the exacting of a higher degree of control by drivers than by individuals in less responsible positions. The essence of the definition is expressed by the following quotation: "If the ability of the driver of an automobile has been lessened in the slightest degree by the use of intoxicating liquors, then the driver is deemed to be under the influence of intoxicating liquor." Nothing could be plainer than this; nor is the enforcement of such a ruling difficult, for as we shall see there is good evidence that a quite moderate level of blood alcohol concentration may be established experimentally at which all individuals, however tolerant to alcohol, will show evidence of lessened neuromuscular co-ordination which may reasonably imply some lessening of their ability to drive a car. As a matter of fact, in order to conform literally to this definition, the minimum blood alcohol concentration might be placed considerably lower than the 150 mg.% now advocated by the National Safety Council (2) as providing *definite* evidence of being under the influence of liquor. There can be no doubt that in the states of Arizona, Iowa, Idaho, Kansas, Massachusetts, Minnesota, Nebraska, New Jersey, Ohio, Pennsylvania, Texas, and Vermont, where this definition holds, the presence of 150 mg.% of alcohol in the blood invariably indicates being under the influence of intoxicating liquor. Whether we consider this as just or not depends to some extent on our philosophy regarding the administration of justice—notably whether we feel that legislation should be directed at some specific and easily determined condition such as the presence of 150 mg.% of alcohol in the blood or the driving of an automobile faster than an arbitrarily established maximum speed limit, or that its direction should be toward an offense against the public welfare such as driving a car less cautiously and skillfully than called for by the standards of the community because of having imbibed of alcohol, or driving dangerously or recklessly regardless of the actual speed involved. Enforcement is undoubtedly more difficult in the latter case; but it seems to us that the extra effort is more than repaid by the higher degree of justice, with consequent respect for the law by the people.

The definition of intoxication prevailing in California is typical of a second group of 5 states, consisting of California, Delaware, Illinois, New York, and Wisconsin. This definition is expressed by the following quotation: "any abnormal mental or physical condition caused by the indulgence in any degree in intoxicating liquor which impairs, to an appreciable degree, the ability of the driver to operate his car in the manner that an *ordinarily* prudent and cautious person, in full possession of his faculties would operate a similar vehicle under like conditions." Strictly speaking, then, in these states, so long as an individual retains the ability to operate his car, not to the very best of his own ability, but in the manner that an ordinarily prudent and cautious person would operate it, he is not guilty of driving while intoxicated. This is a situation far different from that which exists in the states adhering to the Arizona-type definition, where the individual is guilty if he reduces his skill in any degree by the use of alcohol. In the second group it is not enough that he reduce his skill in any degree: he must be so affected as to reduce it to the point where he no longer operates his vehicle in the manner of an ordinarily prudent and cautious person. Manifestly, under this interpretation the degree of driving skill originally possessed by the suspect, as well as his inherent and acquired tolerance to alcohol, will determine at what level of blood alcohol concentration his ability will fall below this required standard. As to the standard of driving ability of an "ordinarily prudent and cautious person," it seems reasonable to assume that it is that degree of ability required for the granting of an operator's license, since it is not likely that the state should license an individual to drive a motor vehicle unless it is convinced that he is ordinarily prudent and cautious. It would thus seem necessary under the law in these states to prove not only that a person had taken alcohol, which may best be done by determining the alcohol content of the body fluids, but that by so doing he has reduced his driving ability, in its broadest sense, below that required for operation of a motor vehicle in his community. No doubt this is more difficult of accomplishment than merely to demonstrate a certain concentration of alcohol in the body; but unless it can be shown that at such a concentration of alcohol any individual, regardless of his driving skill and resistance to alcohol, cannot operate a motor vehicle with the ability possessed by an ordinarily prudent and cautious person—and by this we must include anyone licensed to operate a motor vehicle—such demonstration of blood alcohol concentration cannot in itself constitute proof of intoxication within the meaning of the law. While the level of 150 mg.% advocated by the National Safety Council is, we believe, too high for the states in which the law conforms to the Arizona pattern, it is undoubtedly far too low for the California definition. We will concern ourselves with the evidence supporting this statement later in this chapter.

The remaining 7 states define intoxication in a somewhat less definite manner, tending in general more to the California interpretation. Reference is made to the loss of the "normal" control of one's bodily and mental faculties. Whether the term "normal" refers to the ordinary, sober behavior of that individual or to the standard of behavior ordinarily exhibited by the people of the community is in no way made clear. In another instance reference is made to the "proper" operation of a motor vehicle, again a subject for debate. There seems to be little to be said for definitions such as these, prevailing in Alabama, Arkansas, Georgia, Louisiana, Michigan, Missouri, and North Carolina; and before much progress can be made it seems to us that these states, as well as the larger group possessing no definition at all, must decide on one or the other of the two definitions typified by those of Arizona and California. The National Safety Council champions the former, while we feel that justice is better served by the latter.

Variability of definition.—This variation in the definition of drunkenness in different communities and by different authors has been frequently commented upon but has not, we think, received the consideration it merits. Lauer (3) summarized the situation when he stated the question was "how much must a man drink to render him a dangerous driver?" and added the important qualification: "Some drivers are dangerous without even taking a drink." Bogen (4) noted the variations in the definition of intoxication, while Jetter (5) stated that while an estimate of the amount of alcohol consumed could be made from the blood alcohol concentration, whether or not the individual was drunk depended on the definition.

Alcohol concentration and drunkenness.—In order to appraise the value of chemical tests for intoxication let us review the literature concerning the correlation between alcohol concentration in the body and the degree of drunkenness. We will report in detail those studies in the literature of this country and Great Britain dealing with human subjects. We have already dealt at some length with animal experimentation in this regard, and are inclined not to consider work done on the continent of Europe where standards of driving and administration of justice differ so widely from our own.

Southgate and Carter (6), pharmacologist and police surgeon, respectively, at Sheffield, England, reported in 1926 an investigation of the relationship of blood and urine alcohol concentrations to drunkenness. They noted the ratio between the alcohol content of blood and urine to be 1:1.32, and felt that blood alcohol values could be safely predicted from analysis of urine. They secured urine specimens from 27 inebriates apprehended by the police, and determined the alcohol concentration therein. In 17 of the cases this was over 300 mg.% and in but 3 was it under 200 mg.%. No attempt was made to correlate the alcohol concentrations with the degree of drunkenness, the authors recommending driving tests after the experimental administration of varying doses of alcohol to determine the maximum safe level. They stated on this meager evidence that the alcohol concentration of the blood was the best measure of intoxication.

The first work in this country was reported by Bogen (4, 7, 8) in three papers in 1927 and 1928, all concerned with the same material. He suggested the use of urine or breath rather than blood, because of their more ready availability, and determined experimentally that the alcohol content of 2 liters of air was only slightly greater than that of 1 cc. of urine. Three hundred patients brought to the Cincinnati General Hospital suspected of drunkenness were tested clinically and chemically. A clinical diagnosis of inebriation was made only in the presence of unmistakable loss of control of speech and movement. No patient with less than 1 mg. per cubic centimeter concentration was adjudged intoxicated by the clinical test, while 50% of those with concentrations from 1 to 2 mg., 75% of those with 3 mg., and *almost* all with 4 mg. or above were so diagnosed. Thus there was apparent a very definite tendency for clinical intoxication to be associated with the higher concentrations of alcohol; yet it was equally apparent that, while half of the subjects with concentrations of from 1 to 2 mg. were adjudged drunk, some few individuals with concentrations of more than twice this magnitude were considered sober by the standards used, thus indicating a marked difference in tolerance to alcohol. Bogen was conservative in his appraisal of the procedure, stating: "It is not expected that this test should supersede entirely all the other clinical examinations, but, as any other laboratory procedure, it must be interpreted in the light of the observations in the individual. . . . . most reliable single factor." Although the criteria of drunkenness used by Bogen indicated a more severe degree of incapacitation than that which would be involved in the consideration of motor-vehicle offenses, the variability of different individuals to like concentrations of alcohol existing at this level no doubt prevails throughout the range.

Also in 1927, Gettler and Tiber (9) published a study of

the concentration of alcohol in the brains of alcoholics coming to autopsy. They stated that they had analyzed 6,000 brains; but data were presented on only 32. An endeavor was made to correlate the condition of the patient before death with the brain alcohol concentration; but since many of the individuals died a violent death, which precluded any very objective appraisal of their behavior before its occurrence, such as "hit by train," "hit by auto," "gunshot wound," and so on, one wonders how reliable these observations were. Nevertheless, they stated that in all with brain alcohol below 100 mg.% the behavior of the person had been in all ways normal; from 100 to 250 mg.% there was some "physiological disturbance" but in no case great enough to be noticed by others or described as intoxicated; while all above 250 mg.% were reported as intoxicated. The fact was stressed that the effect of alcohol is due not to the amount consumed but rather to the alcohol content of the brain, a conclusion with which all must agree. Tolerance they believed to be due to increased oxidation of alcohol by habitués, basing their opinion on early German work. Another paper by Gettler (10) two years later presented no new material, but somewhat amplified his conclusions. He noted the difficulty of obtaining adequate histories on his autopsy material, but still concluded: "If there is .25% in the brain, the man becomes unbalanced, whether an habituee or not," thus denying the existence of inherent or acquired tolerance to the presence of alcohol in the brain.

In 1931 Gettler and Freireich (11) studied the relationship between the alcohol concentrations in blood, spinal fluid, and brain in 16 cadavers, as well as the spinal fluid concentration and blood concentration in 15 living inebriates. In the cadavers the spinal fluid concentration was always greater than the brain concentration, the ratio in intoxicated individuals being 1.4 : 1.0 but at low concentrations as high as 3 : 1. This is quite understandable from what we now know about the lag in spinal-fluid alcohol concentration, which would be most apparent at low concentrations. The blood-brain ratio varied widely, from

.66 : 1 to 4.55 : 1. This variation they believed to be due to the different stages of absorption at which death occurred. In the series of 15 living drunks the average spinal fluid concentration was 272 mg.%. From this they concluded that 265 mg.% or higher in the spinal fluid is an index of intoxication. They stated further: "All cases in which the alcohol content of the brain was below 0.2% were not intoxicated." Some of the values of blood and spinal-fluid alcohol found by these workers were indeed remarkable, as noted by Muehlberger (2). Thus the blood alcohol concentration of an intoxicated individual was reported as 1.032%, and a concentration of .695% was found in a subject noted to have a stable equilibrium. These results are so far out of line with those of subsequent investigators as to induce skepticism.

Johnson (12) reported 200 examinations of blood alcohol in admissions for acute alcoholism to the New York Naval Hospital, using Bogen's method. He did not enumerate his criteria of drunkenness on clinical examination, and the results are difficult to evaluate. It was noted that the chemical findings were in practical accord with the clinical picture. At 300 mg.% all were mentally confused, while from 100 to 200 mg.% half were depressed and half exhilarated.

Heise and Halporn (13) in 1932 tried guessing the blood alcohol concentration in 26 cases of acute alcoholism, and then checked their guesses by chemical determinations. In general there was good agreement between the estimated and actual concentrations, but no clinical description of the degree of drunkenness of the subjects was given. The statement, not in accord with subsequent or antecedent work, was made that the alcohol values in whole blood, serum, and plasma are equal. Far more important was the testing of actual driving ability in subjects after the ingestion of from 1 to 5 ounces of whisky. An ingenious if somewhat clumsy method of testing reaction time was used; the firing of a pistol into the road was the signal for the driver to apply the brakes, which fired a second pistol into the road, and from the known speed and the distance between the bullet holes the reaction time could be calculated. The distance traveled at 30 miles per hour between the signal and the application of the brakes increased from 16 to 22 feet, although in no case was the blood alcohol concentration over 100 mg.%. Other tests included steering a course between cardboard boxes, and parking. The authors stated that the results were "too voluminous to record," which is a great pity; for it is just such work that would provide us with the data we so much need. Neither is there any notation of the variation in performances of different individuals when sober. If records of these experiments exist, it is the duty of the authors to publish them in full, since the opportunity for conducting such a study is not easily come by. The results as reported in this paper, and again by Heise (14) in 1934, are not of great value in correlating performance with blood alcohol values; possibly the protocols would provide useful information. Studies of this sort are of much greater value than those involving tests of single skills in the laboratory but require much apparatus and involve no little danger and responsibility. It was the authors' opinion that an obviously drunk driver may suddenly resume his self-control on being confronted with a test situation. What relation this has to the problem it is difficult to say; it seems to us that being confronted with a dangerous situation on the highway would provide a greater incentive to "pull oneself together" than would a laboratory test. One of the findings was of especial interest—that when performance was not affected at routine tasks, unusual or new tasks were poorly done.

Smith and Stewart (15) tested a group of healthy young subjects at Edinburgh University after a dose of 216 cc. of whisky. In this regard it must be remembered that most Scotch whisky for consumption in the United Kingdom is of low concentration of alcohol, actually about 70 proof, so that the dose here was only about 1 cc. per kilogram body weight. Breath and urine alcohol determinations were made, and it was found that during the absorptive phase there was no constant relationship between them. The necessity of taking urine samples at short intervals if the alcohol concentration is to be accurately followed was brought out. Some of the subjects of this investigation were pronounced sober by a police surgeon, and showed no deterioration of ability in certain psychological tests when their urine alcohol was over 200 mg.%. The authors considered the test valueless for the diagnosis of drunkenness but useful as an indication of the minimum amount of alcohol consumed.

Schmidt (16) followed the blood alcohol concentration in the subjects studied by Bahnsen and Vedel-Petersen, and found that in general maximum impairment of performance of the tests of neuromuscular co-ordination occurred about five minutes after the peak of blood alcohol, indicating that in the individual case there was good correlation between performance deficit and blood alcohol concentration.

Thirty-two cases brought into a receiving hospital in Detroit on suspicion of acute alcoholism were studied by Turner (17). Alcohol analyses were run on blood from a cubital vein. His criteria of drunkenness were as follows: "Intoxicated: under the influence of liquor. Able to stand, but walk and talk not normal." This is quite similar to the standard used by Bogen, and probably indicates a degree of intoxication greater than that which would interfere with the safe conduct of a motor vehicle by the average driver. Those subjects showing blood alcohol concentrations of from 100 to 200 mg.% were not adjudged intoxicated, while those with 210 to 300 mg.% were so considered and in about half of these the author felt that the clinical examination showed a greater degree of intoxication than was revealed by the blood test, again indicating a difference in tolerance of different individuals. He concluded: "In general, intoxication is not noticeable in the human until the blood alcohol concentration is greater than .2%."

The *British Medical Journal* in 1937 (18) reported a German study by Hoffmann which is worthy of note because of the large series of cases involved. Some 2,500 drivers of motor vehicles were examined and classified clinically, as sober, slightly affected, and definitely intoxicated; the actual criteria were not mentioned. Blood alcohol determinations were made on all of them, and of the 750 with blood alcohol concentrations below 100 mg.% only 10 were definitely intoxicated, while of the 250 with concentrations over 200 mg.% only 19 were sober. Striking individual variation was noted, however, 3 with less than 40 mg.% being diagnosed as definitely intoxicated and 5 with over 240 mg.% showing no signs of alcoholism. Thus it was seen that some individuals were more affected by one "large whisky" than were others by six times this amount, indicating a definite tolerance of the brain to alcohol. It was felt, however, that the test provided a fairly accurate gauge of the minimum amount drunk by the subject.

Probably the best-controlled study of the correlation of drunkenness with alcohol concentration is that of Jetter (19), who examined 1,150 patients brought to the hospital on suspicion of alcoholism. Blood alcohol determinations were run by Heise's method, and the clinical diagnosis made on certain definite criteria. Thus there must have been present, first, gross gait abnormality or inability to walk, and, second, at least two of the following signs: gross abnormality of speech or inability to talk, flushed face, dilated pupils, or odor of alcohol on the breath. The author noted that the fulfillment of these criteria indicated a rather pronounced degree of drunkenness but felt that making them less stringent would detract from the objectivity of the experiment. Of the subjects 150 showed no alcohol in the blood, while in 740 a clinical diagnosis of inebriation was made. The percentage intoxicated at each level of blood alcohol concentration was enumerated as follows: 5–75 mg.% blood alcohol, 10.5% intoxicated; 75–125 mg., 18.5%; 125–175 mg., 47%; 175–225 mg., 83.6%; 225–275 mg., 90%; 275–325 mg., 95.1%; 325–375 mg., 96.0%; 375–425 mg., 93.3%; and over 425 mg., 100%. It can be seen quite readily that although the general correlation is definite, a great deal of individual variation in tolerance must exist to account for those individuals called drunk at low blood alcohol levels as well as those designated as sober at very high levels. Nor is the evidence of variation in tolerance in any way invalidated by the stringent criteria of drunkenness employed, although any conclusions regarding the safe level of blood alcohol for motor-vehicle operation on the basis of these data must be made with this in mind.

Jetter (20) also gave alcohol experimentally to a group of normal young adults in doses of from 1 to 2 cc. per kilogram. Samples of venous blood were examined at intervals thereafter, and the blood alcohol values so obtained were compared with the presence or absence of drunkenness, using the same criteria as in the previous study. In the individual case the greatest degree of intoxication coincided with the maximum blood alcohol concentration, in agreement with the work of Schmidt (16). The incidence of drunkenness at the different levels of blood alcohol was as follows: 75–125 mg., 50%; 125–175 mg., 57%; 175–225 mg., 100%. It is at once apparent that these individuals showed a greater degree of drunkenness at a given level of blood alcohol than did the hospital patients. Jetter advanced the possible explanation that the reason for this was that these subjects were abstainers or occasional drinkers, while the hospital patients were presumably habituated to alcohol. Another possibility is that, since the experimental subjects were tested during the absorptive phase, their arterial blood alcohol and brain alcohol concentrations were actually higher than the venous blood concentrations indicated. Further, we have Mellanby's observation, since confirmed, that the degree of drunkenness is greater at the same blood alcohol concentration when this is increasing than when it is decreasing. Thus this observation of Jetter's cannot be accepted as definite proof of the existence of acquired tolerance to alcohol, much as it suggests it. In a later paper (5) these findings were summarized and the statement was made that because of this variation in tolerance the chemical test should be supplemented by clinical examination. He was, however, willing to accept the limit of 150 mg.% proposed by the National Safety Council as definite evidence of intoxication from the standpoint of motor-vehicle operation.

Harger, Lamb, and Hulpieu (21), in a paper devoted largely to the presentation of evidence that determination of alcohol in the expired air is a valid indication of the concentration in the blood, reported tests on 140 individuals in hospital, many of whom had been involved in accidents. Clinical findings were noted by an interne and were unknown to the persons running the determinations of blood and breath alcohol. None of those with concentrations of less than 50 mg.% were clinically diagnosed as "under the influence," while 46% of those with 50 to 100 mg.%, 50% with 100 to 150 mg.%, 92% with 150 to 200 mg.%, and all with over 200 mg.% were so diagnosed. No criteria for the clinical diagnosis of intoxication were listed, but the figures would indicate that these authors interpreted "under the influence" in a less strict sense than Bogen, Turner, and Jetter did in regard to "intoxication." From this evidence, and that in the literature, they concluded that 150 mg.% of alcohol in the blood or its equivalent in the breath should constitute prima facie evidence of being under the influence of intoxicating liquor.

Selesnick (22), in a review of the subject, noted his experience with 50 patients admitted to Boston City Hospital for acute alcoholism. He stated that except for the odor of alcohol on the breath, clinical manifestations of intoxication did not appear until the blood alcohol concentration reached 200 mg.%. From 200 to 300 mg.% there were definite changes in affect and some difficulty with locomotion. He felt, however, that subclinical intoxication was the important thing so far as motor-vehicle operation was concerned, and that for the purpose of demonstrating the presence of this rather theoretical state blood alcohol examination was of value.

Morgan reported (23) his experience based on 125 alcohol

determinations made for medicolegal purposes. In 86 cases the alcohol was determined in the urine, in 39 in the blood, and in 8 in both blood and urine. The average urine alcohol was 272 mg.%, and the average blood alcohol 210 mg.%, which he took to indicate that the police seldom charge a man with intoxication who is not grossly drunk, a conclusion that might be taken exception to. The suspects were examined by the police and by a physician as well. In no case did the result of the test disagree with the report of the physician, and in but one case with that of the police and here there was no alcohol in the blood and the suspect was freed. The level of blood or urine alcohol at which a chemical diagnosis of drunkenness was made was not specifically stated; but since the author does make the statement that in his opinion no person with a blood alcohol concentration over 75 mg.% should drive, in want of anything more definite we may assume that this was the limit chosen. With this low limit, and the knowledge that these people were brought in charged with intoxication by the police, it is little wonder that no disagreement existed between the chemical diagnosis and the police opinion; in fact, the lower the concentration limit set the less disagreement we should expect, for it is obvious that the police would not have brought them in unless they were convinced they were intoxicated. Such a study therefore proves very little one way or the other.

An experimental study on a small group of subjects was published by Lauer (24), using special testing equipment designed to evaluate those attributes necessary to safe driving. Blood alcohol determinations were made during the tests. He used 4 subjects: 2 physicians who did not drink and an engineer of the same drinking habits, all of whom were about 30 years of age; and a 46-year-old war veteran who was suspected of taking moderate amounts of alcohol on occasion. Two practice tests were given before the procedure, but even this he felt was not enough to eliminate the learning curve. Why he did not carry on the practice to the point of accomplishing this he did not state, and one wonders whether this may not be a convenient explanation for results not entirely in accord with what he expected. In each case a battery of 5 tests was run through, and then 2½ ounces of whisky diluted to 200 cc. with water was given, with repetition of the tests at the end of 30 minutes. This was repeated sequentially twice in three of the subjects and once in the fourth, the whisky having run out by the time his turn came. Performance in the tests was rated not on an absolute scale but in relation to initial performance—a questionable procedure if we are to accept performance on the tests as a criterion of driving ability, which is what they were designed for. At any rate, at the end of the experiment one subject with a blood alcohol of 125 mg.% showed a drop in efficiency to −71.9, another with 111 mg.% to −103, and a third with 118 mg.% to −87. This last subject a half-hour earlier at a blood alcohol concentration of but 67 mg.% had shown a much greater drop, to −140.1—certainly not a very convincing demonstration of correlation between blood alcohol and test performance. The moderately alcoholic war veteran attained a concentration of 74 mg.%, and showed a slight increase in performance, amounting to only +.44. If he is to be compared with one of the teetotal subjects with a loss to −140.1 at a slightly lower blood alcohol concentration, one must indeed be impressed with the tolerance to be gained from moderate drinking. Obviously the series is too small, and the data presented are too few, to permit one to draw any very valid conclusions from this work, which, in common with too great a proportion of the papers dealing with this subject, has the aspect more of a moral lecture than of a scientific investigation.

Bavis (25) recently reported the relationship between the urine alcohol concentration and the clinical state of intoxication in 120 individuals charged with drunken driving. The degree of intoxication was rated as not influenced, slightly influenced, moderately influenced, and strongly influenced. There was but 1 case with urine alcohol below 100 mg.%, which was considered not influenced. From 110 to 200 mg.%, 1 case was not influenced, 67% were slightly influenced, and 27% were moderately influenced. From 210 to 300 mg.%, 1 case was not influenced, 11% were slightly influenced, and 88% were moderately influenced. Above 310 mg.%, 1 case was not influenced, none were slightly influenced, and 94% were moderately influenced, while 2 cases were strongly influenced. Here again we see a good general correlation of drunkenness with alcohol concentration; but the equally important exceptions to the rule indicative of variation in tolerance are no less obvious. Bavis invoked the oft-repeated explanation of the sobering influence of the examination to account for some of those exceptions but was forced to admit that this did not completely explain the seeming extraordinary tolerance of the occasional individual. He was of the opinion, however, that since these individuals also were involved in accidents they were equally guilty of the offense of drunken driving. Until he is able to prove in some objective manner that such an individual is unable to exercise ordinary ability in operating a motor vehicle, other than the simple fact that he was so unfortunate as to be involved in an accident, we must remain unconvinced.

The Stanford University School of Medicine and the Division of Drivers' Licenses of the Department of Motor Vehicles, State of California, have been engaged in an experimental study of the relation of alcohol concentration to driving abilities, in an endeavor to work out some practicable yet just method for apprehending and convicting those individuals who present a hazard on the road because of indulgence in alcohol and—even more important—to provide unbiased factual data for use in educating the driving public to a realization of the dangers of drinking and driving. The first of this work has been published by Newman and Fletcher (26), and was concerned with the correlation between blood alcohol concentration and ability to perform certain acts involved in motor-vehicle operation as tested by equipment used by the Division of Drivers' Licenses in the examination of special groups of drivers. Performance on this testing apparatus had been found to correlate well with driving ability, although it was recognized that poor performance on the tests was compatible with safe driving if the driver was aware of and remained within his limitations. Two tests were used. The first, which was termed "Simple Braking," was scored as the number of centiseconds required for the subject to apply the brakes after a red light flashed on. The second, "Simple Steering," was recorded as the percentage of a one-minute period during which the subject, by manipulation of a conventional steering wheel, was able to maintain the alignment of two objects on a screen within a tolerance of one-quarter inch, one of these objects being in constant irregular motion beyond the subject's control, and the other actuated by the steering wheel. When the two tests were performed simultaneously, the procedure was termed "Vigilance Steering and Braking." The braking test was designed to measure reaction time and the steering test eye-to-hand co-ordination, while the combined test introduced complexity and the factor of attention. A certain amount of judgment was involved in all, but particularly in the combined test. Nevertheless, the investigators were well aware of the desirability of a better test of judgment, and acknowledged the handicap involved by the lack of such a test.

A period of practice on a day prior to the examination was found to control fairly adequately the effect of practice, subsequent scores not varying more than 5% on either side of the base line. Thus changes greater than this in magnitude must have been due to the effect of alcohol. On the day of the examination the subject presented himself at the laboratory, having not eaten for at least three hours, and a control score on the tests was secured. He was then given a dose of alcohol varying from 0.5 to 2 cc. per kilogram as either Scotch or Bourbon whisky diluted with soda water and cooled with ice, which he was expected to ingest within 15 minutes. In the great majority of cases the dose was 1 cc. per kilogram, the other doses being given in repetitions of the test on the same subjects. At the end of an hour after the start of imbibition the tests were given again, and a sample of venous blood from a cubital vein was obtained for analysis for alcohol by the method described by Newman. The blood alcohol concentrations at the time of the test varied from 45 to 185 mg.%, the peak of the distribution curve being at 100 mg.%.

In spite of the homogeneity of the group tested, the scores on the tests varied rather widely, this variation being slightly less in the more complex steering tests than in the braking reaction time. Thus in the steering test the range of scores before alcohol was from 99.2 to 65.5%, a spread of 33.7%, while the greatest drop recorded after alcohol was slightly less than this, from 78.5 to 48%, or 30.5%. In the braking test the range of scores before alcohol was from 36.1 to 53.3 centiseconds, a spread of 17.2 centiseconds, while the greatest decrease in performance after alcohol was slightly more than this, 18.4 centiseconds. Because of this very considerable variation in performance from person to person, which probably correlates well with their skill if not necessarily with their safeness as operators of motor vehicles, it must at once be obvious that even if all the subjects were affected in the same degree by a given concentration of alcohol in the blood their performance after alcohol would vary much as it had before, the general level being lowered but the variations from one individual to another remaining. This is merely another expression of the commonly accepted fact that drivers vary in their skill, so that if all were to suffer an equal loss of skill some would be reduced below the accepted minimum standard while others, although less skillful than formerly, would still be above average.

In addition to this, it was found that the loss in skill by different individuals at the same blood alcohol concentration was not equal, but varied within wide limits, as had been indicated by other workers already quoted. In demonstrating this fact, the data from 98 trials on 65 subjects were considered.

The test of "Vigilance Steering and Braking" was used as the criterion of driving skill, since it embodied more factors common to this than either test taken separately, although the same conclusions could be reached by the use of the data on either "Simple Steering" or "Simple Braking." Drop in performance after alcohol in each component of the test was calculated as the percentage of the original score represented by the difference in the scores before and after alcohol. This percentage drop in the two components was averaged to give the final figure used in the survey. It should be noted that this value gave a valid measure of loss of skill for comparison within the members of the group, but did not in any way represent any concrete "amount of skill," if such could be conceived. To illustrate: a man showing for example a drop of 50% would be affected twice as much as one showing a drop of 25%, but one could not by any means say that this meant that he had exactly 50% of his original skill remaining after alcohol.

The correlation between this loss of skill on the tests and the blood alcohol concentration at the time of the test was calculated for the whole group by the Pearson correlation-coefficient formula, in which a coefficient of 1.0 indicates perfect and 0.0 no correlation. The value determined was 0.485. When it is recalled that a similar correlation, namely 0.5, exists between the height and weight of a population, it readily will be seen that the correlation between blood alcohol concentration and loss of ability on the tests was far from perfect. True, those with high blood alcohol concentrations did tend to show the greatest losses, just as tall people tend to weigh more than short ones; yet we must admit that a yardstick makes a rather crude weighing machine. So also we must consider blood alcohol concentration a crude indicator of the degree of intoxication.

No attempt was made to deduce from the data the blood alcohol concentration at which an individual, or even the average individual, could be considered under the influence of alcohol so far as motor-vehicle operation is concerned. In order to apply the findings to this problem, we must first accept one of the various definitions of the terms "under the influence" or "intoxicated," and then satisfy ourselves concerning the validity of the tests used in gauging the ability to safely conduct a motor vehicle. As to the definition: If the Arizona definition is used, all the tests need show is that some impairment, however slight, has occurred due to alcohol and it can be safely assumed that any change in score beyond the maximum chance variation of 5% indicated such impairment. Then the blood alcohol concentration at which all subjects tested showed impairment in excess of this 5% should constitute definite evidence of being under the influence of alcohol. The data of Newman and Fletcher show this to occur at approximately 105 mg.%. We may therefore say without fear of contradiction that this work indicates that when the blood alcohol concentration exceeds 105 mg.% all individuals are in some degree affected by alcohol. That this concentration might well be placed considerably lower by the use of more sensitive tests is quite possible; and it must further be borne in mind that many individuals would show this degree of impairment at concentrations of half this magnitude. Thus it is seen that the evidence of this work supports the validity of a blood alcohol concentration considerably lower than that laid down by the National Safety Council as prima facie evidence of being "under the influence" in those states subscribing to the Arizona type definition. As for the states interpreting the term in the California fashion, the problem is not so simple. To be of positive value in this regard, the tests employed must be capable of determining whether or not an individual can drive a motor vehicle in the manner in which an ordinarily prudent and cautious person would operate a similar vehicle under the same circumstances. We believe the tests capable of evaluating skill in certain restricted activities necessary to motor-vehicle operation, but certainly proficiency in this restricted sphere of activity is no guarantee of safe conduct of a car. As a matter of fact, one individual with half the skill of another as recorded by the tests may be the safer driver, if he recognizes his limitations and remains within them. Also, the tests are not adequate in the evaluation of the more abstract factors contributing to safe driving, such as judgment and caution. Thus we cannot say that there is a certain score on these tests which represents the minimum skill compatible with safe driving, and that the blood alcohol concentration at which all subjects fell below this minimum should be considered prima facie evidence of intoxication. Should it be possible to develop such a test, which could be shown to correlate with ability to drive a motor car with safety, then the problem of licensing drivers would be solved, and when an individual showed himself to fall below the standard set, because of the presence of alcohol in his blood in any significant amount, a conviction for drunken driving could easily be obtained under the California ruling. In the absence of such a test we must rely on the behavior of the individual as indicated by the evidence of how he was driving at the time of the accident, supported by the usual clinical examination for drunkenness, which might well be improved by the use of testing equipment such as was employed in this study, incomplete as is the information so obtained.

Further work is being carried on by the same investigators in an attempt to develop a battery of tests that will provide a valid estimate of the safety of drivers of motor vehicles and to determine the effect of varying concentrations of blood alcohol on performance in these tests. This, it seems, is the most rational approach to the problem. Work has already been done on the effect of alcohol on certain of the special senses; and it was found that visual acuity, distance judgment, ocular fusion, field of vision, resistance to and recovery from glare, and hearing were affected in different degree at the same blood alcohol concentration. It was of interest that the greater the number of different test procedures the more subjects showed changes in at least one of them. This supports the contention that a battery of tests is more valuable than any one used alone.

Another obstacle in the path of the chemical diagnosis of drunkenness is the observation, made as early as 1919 by Mellanby, that the effect of the same concentration of alcohol while this is rising is greater than when it is on the decline. This has been confirmed and amplified by two recent communications. Mirsky and his co-workers (32) noted the disappearance of the symptoms of intoxication in rabbits after rapid intravenous injection of alcohol, in spite of the fact that removal of the liver had preceded the injection with the result that the blood alcohol concentration remained constant over a considerable period. Using human subjects, they found that if drunkenness were induced by a single large dose, and then blood alcohol was maintained constant by subsequent smaller doses, the symptoms of intoxication cleared up in a few hours in spite of the constant blood alcohol concentration. If another dose equal to the initial one was then given, the symptoms were no more severe than after the first dose, in spite of the fact that the blood alcohol concentration was much higher. From this the authors concluded that the central nervous system is able in time to adapt itself to concentrations of alcohol that if attained rapidly would induce marked intoxication. Independently and almost contemporaneously Eggleton (33) came to essentially the same conclusions, using human subjects and appraising the degree of intoxication by psychological tests. She felt that the degree of intoxication was more dependent on the rate of increase of the blood alcohol concentration than on its absolute value. We have confirmed the work of these authors in a preliminary survey in this laboratory.

From the foregoing observations, it becomes apparent that in order to predict the degree of drunkenness that any individual will show at a given blood alcohol concentration, we must not only know the subject's inherent and acquired tolerance to alcohol but must also be in possession of information regarding the trend of his blood alcohol curve at the time, since this will in large measure determine the intoxicant effect. Some information in this regard can be obtained from a careful history regarding when the alcohol was ingested, and in what relation to meals. However, this can be only an approximation. So we see that the factor of time after imbibition enters into all of the experimental work we have reported, and introduces a complication that prevents its absolute application in the clinical sphere.

Validity of fixed limits of alcohol concentration.—This, then, is the evidence that has been collected in the past fifteen years on which we must base our appraisal of the chemical diagnosis of drunkenness. Certain of the data are directly applicable to the problem, and were obtained in a manner sufficiently objective to leave little doubt of their validity. In all of the work done on patients brought into hospitals suspected of drunkenness, the criteria of drunkenness were so strict as to make valid the contention that if less stringent criteria, such as would be applicable to motor-vehicle operation, had been adopted the blood alcohol concentration at which intoxication would have been universal might have been considerably lower. These studies did, however, provide irrefutable evidence of the variability of tolerance to alcohol among a group of individuals. The fact that these studies showed a *majority* of individuals to be drunk by the criteria employed at the level of blood alcohol of 150 mg.% is, however, no proof that *all* would have shown the lesser degree of intoxication which would endanger motor-vehicle operation at the same concentration. Certainly there can be no argument that it is necessary, if we set a certain concentration of blood alcohol as prima facie evidence of intoxication, that all, not just a majority, must show some demonstrable though not necessarily marked evidence of intoxication at this concentration. This had not been demonstrated for the 150 mg.% concentration sponsored by the National Safety Council until publication of the work of Newman and Fletcher (26), and it is their work actually which validates this concentration as prima facie evidence of drunkenness in those states subscribing to the Arizona interpretation of the term "under the influence." By the same token, there is no evidence at all in existence supporting such a concentration as prima facie evidence of intoxication in states which adhere to the definition as expressed in California; and such a concentration, or even a much higher one, could not be considered as definite evidence of intoxication in these states without other supporting evidence unless a change in the law or its interpretation were brought about.

Question of stricter interpretation of intoxication.—Whether such a change is desirable is a debatable point. There can be no doubt that alcohol is a potent factor in the causation of accidents. A thorough if somewhat partisan review of this matter is that of Berry (27) of the National Safety Council. He felt that official figures usually underestimated the percentage of accidents in which alcohol probably played a part, while special studies tended to comprise too few cases to be statistically valid, and that a safe compromise was about 20% for the incidence of drinking in drivers and pedestrians involved in fatal accidents, with a slightly lower figure in nonfatal accidents. He quoted in extenso the work of Holcomb (31), who had determined the blood alcohol concentration in 1,750 drivers of motor vehicles not involved in accidents as well as in a group of drivers in personal injury accidents. Of the first group 12% and of the second 47% showed alcohol in the blood, while there were 33 times as many of those involved in accidents with over 150 mg.% as of nonaccident drivers. He calculated that an individual with 150 mg.% of alcohol in the blood had 55 times as great a chance of meeting with an accident as one free of alcohol. These data indicate graphically the importance of the problem of drunken driving, and the necessity for improvement in the situation, both by educating the driving public to a realization of the danger involved and by apprehending and bringing to justice those who fail to profit from the educational campaign.

No matter how active the police may be in apprehending the drunken driver, or how easy his conviction is made, real and lasting progress in the solution of the problem must depend on education of public opinion. In this connection, it is important that no step be taken in enforcement of the law which will tend to prejudice public opinion unfavorably, as we think there can be no doubt it has been influenced in regard to arbitrary speed limits, and as there can be no possible doubt it was in relation to the Eighteenth Amendment. It has been established experimentally, as we have noted, that all individuals are affected in some degree by the blood alcohol concentration of 150 mg.% advanced by the National Safety Council, and that therefore they are guilty, if in charge of a motor vehicle, of driving under the influence of alcohol in those states following the Arizona definition of this term or in any other state that deems it advisable to change the law to conform to that definition. It has not, in our opinion, been in any manner established that a certain considerable number of individuals may not be able to drive a car in a manner no more dangerous than the standards prescribed in their community with this amount of alcohol in their blood. Their sole offense would be, therefore, the presence of alcohol in the blood; this would be apparent not only to them but to their associates and all who observed their arrest and trial, and the resultant disrespect for what might well be interpreted as a harsh and unjust statute would negate any educational campaign that might be instituted. For this very important reason we feel it advisable to direct the punitive effort of the law against the individual who, because of drinking, drives his car in an unsafe manner, rather than against those whose only offense may consist of a blood alcohol concentration of 150 mg.%. The definition of intoxication prevailing in California is the best safeguard of this application of justice, and there seems to be every reason for retaining it. Under these circumstances the determination of alcohol concentration may be very valuable as supporting evidence and may be given the force of fact regarding the minimum amount of alcohol consumed, without in itself constituting prima facie evidence of the offense.

Somewhat in contrast to the enthusiasm of the proponents of the chemical diagnosis of drunkenness are the opinions of certain writers who have reviewed the evidence on the subject. McGrath (28) covered the literature very completely and came to the conclusion that the concentration of alcohol in the blood was much better evidence of the degree of drunkenness than the amount of alcohol consumed. He declared himself, however, against hard and fast limits of concentration, and suggested rather that the concentration found be presented to the court, with interpretive information as to the percentage of individuals who would be drunk at that concentration, and that this information be considered in relation to the other evidence in the case. In summary, he stated it was "evident that blood alcohol estimation does not provide an automatic answer to the question, Was the individual drunk?"

Cameron (29), in an address before the City of Winnipeg Advisory Traffic Commission, noted that: "The majority of the scientific papers [dealing with the relation of blood alcohol to ability to drive] give a reasonably dispassionate treatment of the subject, but occasional papers, reports, and books suggest an atmosphere reminiscent of the supposed slogan of the R.C.M.P.—they seem out to 'get their man'." He concluded that tests of blood alcohol concentration should not be rigidly interpreted to indicate whether or not a person was under the influence of alcohol but should properly be used as additional contributory evidence, unless of course no alcohol at all was present, in which case the evidence would be absolute.

While the desirability of changes in the law regarding driving while under the influence of alcohol, especially as regards the definition of that term, may properly be a topic for philosophical discussion, the actual practical problem of the application of chemical tests for drunkenness is more concrete and factual in nature, and may be summarized very briefly. In the light of the evidence at hand, in those states which adhere to the definition typified by Arizona, there can be no doubt that a concentration of alcohol in the blood of 150 mg. %, or even considerably less, is a definite and positive indication of being under the influence of liquor and can stand alone and unsupported by corroborative evidence. On the other hand, in those states defining intoxication in accord with the California definition, sufficient evidence is not at hand to indicate a minimal concentration at which all individuals could be considered intoxicated, and the chemical diagnosis of drunkenness must be confined to an indication of the minimum amount of alcohol the suspect has consumed, with admission of expert testimony as to the effect of this amount on the average individual.

Choice of material for analysis.—Admitting, as we feel we must, that determination of the alcohol concentration of the body fluids provides valuable information regarding the probability of alcohol playing a part in motor-vehicle offenses, it is of the utmost importance that procedures be selected which will give the most information and which are the least subject to error. A primary consideration in this respect is the choice of material for analysis, which has been the subject of many lengthy discussions. The lack of unanimity of opinion is at least partly due to the fact that several factors, rather than one, are operating. Thus desirability may be gauged on a basis of absolute reliability of the result, or again on the ease of obtaining the specimen, or even the simplicity of the analytical procedure that is applicable.

There is no doubt that it is the concentration of alcohol in the brain itself that is responsible for inebriation; and it is equally apparent that this is available for analysis only when a fatal outcome has resulted. In such cases analysis of the brain provides unequivocal information, and is preferable to analysis of any other organ or fluid.

Spinal fluid.—Because of its intimate topographical relationship to the brain, the cerebrospinal fluid has been advocated by Gettler and Freireich (11). They supported their choice by experimental data showing a spinal-fluid-to-brain ratio, which was much more constant than the blood-to-brain ratio, the experiments being performed on cadavers dying during an alcoholic debauch. The validity of these data is open to question, as we have noted already, because of inclusion of values of concentration which far exceed those accepted as compatible with life. Moreover, the intimacy of relationship between the brain and the lumbar spinal fluid is more apparent than real, and presents nothing to compare with the surface for diffusion that exists between the blood in the cerebral capillaries and the brain substance. We have seen how far from accurately the lumbar-fluid concentration follows the cisternal-fluid concentration, and how closely this latter follows the blood. When we add to this the practical impossibility of securing such specimens in other than a well-equipped hospital, we understand the lack of popularity of this fluid for the diagnosis of drunkenness.

Blood.—Blood probably reflects the concentration of alcohol in the brain more accurately than any other obtainable material, and has been the standard of reference for them all. It presents no particular difficulty in analysis, and is easily stored and transported. Without a doubt, were it not for the inconvenience and legal obstacles to its procurement, all authorities would be in accord on its acceptance. From the standpoint of the technical difficulty of securing blood samples, it must be granted that a physician or trained technician is required. Since we feel that in every case of suspected intoxication examination by a physician is equally if not more important than the alcohol determination, this should not be a very valid obstacle, although no doubt it would entail some effort on the part of the police. From the legal aspect, the consent of the suspect is as necessary for the securing of specimens of saliva or urine as for blood; and there is some precedent for making the submission of a sample mandatory in recent decisions regarding blood grouping for the determination of paternity. There can be no very real objection to the interpretation that while compulsory blood alcohol determinations compel the suspect to provide evidence which may be used against him, this evidence is factual and unprejudiciable in nature, and no amount of coercion can change it in the slightest degree. Thus the freedom of the individual from the threat of obtaining false evidence by coercion is not jeopardized and the administration of justice is expedited. If compulsion is to be allowed, then certainly blood specimens may be obtained with relatively greater ease than could specimens of urine, saliva, or even breath; and the only possible objection to using blood would be the necessity of a physician to obtain the specimen, a requirement that we feel would be very desirable from other considerations. As a matter of fact, blood specimens have been used more widely than any others, notably in Scandinavia and Central Europe.

Urine.—Urine has the advantage of being available with the co-operation of the patient without the need for a specially trained person to collect the sample. It may also be obtained without the subject's knowledge by resorting to subterfuge. From the standpoint of reliability, Bogen (4) found good agreement between the urine and the spinal-fluid concentrations, and there is no lack of work showing a fairly constant relationship between urine and blood concentration in experimental alcoholism. This ratio of alcohol concentrations in blood and urine has been generally agreed on as 1:1.35. However, Haggard and his coworkers (30) have produced evidence that casts serious doubt on the validity of urine determinations in the practical diagnosis of drunkenness. Contrary to the statement of Heise and Halporn (13), that "if subject fails to void, his urinary alcohol disappears just the same, the alcohol being reabsorbed by the blood," they found that subjects, who ingested whisky and retained their urine overnight, in the morning showed no alcohol in the blood but a considerable concentration in the urine. Similarly, alcohol in a concentration of 0.2 to 0.4% instilled into the bladder showed a loss by absorption of but 5 to 7% in a 2-hour period. They found that the agreement between curves of blood and urine alcohol after a test dose of 250 cc. of whisky given by mouth to normal males depended largely on the frequency with which specimens were taken. With longer intervals between specimens there was a very poor correlation between the two curves, while with short periods this was good. Heise and Halporn (13) have reported that drunks usually welcome an opportunity to urinate, indicating that their bladders are usually full. Under these conditions it is apparent from the work of Haggard *et al.* that the concentration in the bladder urine so obtained may well represent the average concentration of the past several hours rather than that prevailing at the time of securing the specimen. A more reliable procedure would be to require emptying of the bladder, with collection of a specimen a short time later. Here, however, the procedure would be complicated by the necessity of securing the suspect's co-operation on two separate occasions, on the second of which he would no longer have the incentive of an uncomfortably full bladder to urge him to comply.

Saliva.—Saliva reflects quite accurately the concentration of alcohol in the blood and of all fluids is probably the simplest to analyze. Its collection, however, requires more than a little co-operation on the part of the subject, as anyone who has tried to produce an adequate sample for experimental work can testify, while the possibility of contamination is greater than in the case of either blood or urine. Either alcohol remaining in the mouth from recent imbibition or eructation of alcohol from the stomach may seriously affect the accuracy of the determination. Since it would be practically impossible from the legal standpoint to rule out these possibilities, evidence from saliva would be of little value.

Breath.—Bogen (4) first proposed the use of breath in the chemical diagnosis of drunkenness, bubbling a known volume through a dichromate solution and determining the amount reduced by the alcohol colorimetrically. He found good agreement between urine and breath alcohol values, 2 liters of breath containing approximately the same amount of alcohol as 1 cc. of urine. Smith and Stewart (15) employed essentially the same method in experimental subjects, and found poor correlation in many cases between blood and breath concentrations. They showed conclusively, by having the same subject vary the depth of his breathing, that the concentration in the breath was very dependent on the depth of breathing, and consequently the amount of alveolar air in the specimen. Thus shallow breathing gave much lower concentrations than did deep breathing. From this they concluded that breath was an unreliable material for alcohol analysis. Harger and his coworkers (21) have borne this in mind in devising their apparatus for the determination of breath alcohol. They determined both the carbon dioxide and the alcohol in the breath. Since the alveolar carbon-dioxide tension is quite constant, the amount of carbon dioxide present indicates the amount of alveolar air in the sample, and the alcohol found can be related to this, circumventing the possibility of changes due to different depths of breathing. By this method they were able to show a very close correlation between blood and breath alcohol. The method has the added advantage of not requiring the co-operation of the suspect, for aspiration through the apparatus, which has the unfortunate appellation of "drunkometer," with the intake in the suspect's breath stream is sufficient to effect a determination. It is said that this apparatus may be successfully used by the highway patrolman, so that determinations may be made on the spot of the accident—a considerable advantage. This method seems to possess numerous virtues for practical use. Just how real these are is problematical, however. The fact that the determination may be made immediately is not of such great importance when one considers that certainly not more than an hour would ordinarily elapse before the suspect could be brought to hospital or police station where blood might be taken. As we have mentioned before, the lack of necessity of a physician to take the sample may be no real advantage, since early examination by a physician is a very important part of the diagnostic procedure. That the method is less reliable than the determination in the blood cannot be in doubt, nor could it be established beyond a doubt that eructation of alcoholic stomach contents into the mouth did not prejudice the result. Particularly in those states in which 150 mg. % of alcohol is accepted as prima facie evidence of driving while under the influence of liquor, the possibilities of a miscarriage of justice due to the lesser reliability of the breath determination would seem to far outweigh its possible advantages. As a matter of fact the responsibility placed on the technician who runs the analysis in these states is very considerable, and only by the greatest of care and avoidance of all possible complicating factors can any reasonable assurance of reliability be gained.

Method of analysis.—It would thus seem that blood is the most satisfactory material for alcohol analysis when all points of view are considered. If urine is used, the bladder must be emptied and a short interval allowed to elapse before the specimen is taken. Breath analysis has the advantage of simplicity, but must be considered less reliable, while saliva has no apparent place in the legal diagnosis of drunkenness. The methods employed for the actual analysis depend on oxidation of the alcohol after it is removed from the specimen by volatilization and determination of the amount of oxidant consumed in the process, by either colorimetry or titration. There are many methods described, all of which are of sufficient accuracy in capable hands. In general, their accuracy varies inversely with their simplicity. None of them is sufficiently simple or foolproof to be trusted to an untrained person. Indeed, if any high degree of accuracy is to be attained, the technician must be trained in the procedure over a considerable time. The results of the analyses are of such great import, especially where they are allowed to convict unsupported by other evidence, that the people have the right to demand every possible safeguard of skill and precaution against error. Even then, the nature of the procedures is such as to preclude absolute assurance against error. It is well to bear this in mind in evaluating the wisdom of legislation which will allow such an error to lodge an innocent man in jail.

REFERENCES

1. National Safety Council, *Progress Report of the Committee on Tests for Intoxication of the Street and Highway Traffic Section,* 1937
2. National Safety Council, *Progress Report of the Committee on Tests for Intoxication of the Street and Highway Traffic Section,* 1940
3. Lauer, A. R., "Effects of Alcohol on Driving," *J. Iowa State Med. Soc.,* **29**:282, 1939
4. Bogen, E., "Drunkenness: a Quantitative Study of Acute Alcoholic Intoxication," *J. Am. Med. Assoc.,* **89**:1508, 1927
5. Jetter, W. W., "Chemical and Clinical Diagnosis of Acute Alcoholism," *New Engl. J. Med.,* **221**:1019, 1939
6. Southgate, H. W., and Carter, G., "Excretion of Alcohol in the Urine as a Guide to Alcoholic Intoxication," *Brit. Med. J.,* **1**:463, 1926
7. Bogen, E., "Diagnosis of Drunkenness—a Quantitative Study of Acute Alcoholic Intoxication," *Calif. and Western Med.,* **26**:778, 1927
8. Bogen, E., "Drunkenness: a Quantitative Study of Acute Alcoholic Intoxication," *Am. J. Med. Sci.,* **176**:153, 1928
9. Gettler, A. O., and Tiber, A., "The Alcoholic Content of the Human Brain: Its Relation to Intoxication," *Arch. Path. Lab. Med.,* **3**:218, 1927
10. Gettler, A. O., "Chemical Evidences of Alcoholic Intoxication and Their Medicolegal Significance," *New Engl. J. Med.,* **201**:725, 1929
11. Gettler, A. O., and Freireich, A. W., "Determination of Alcoholic Intoxication during Life by Spinal Fluid Analysis," *J. Biol. Chem.,* **92**:199, 1931
12. Johnson, F. S., "Report of 200 Examinations for Acute Alcoholism Made at the New York Naval Hospital, New York," *U.S. Naval Med. Bull.,* **28**:85, 1930
13. Heise, H. A., and Halporn, B., "Medicolegal Aspects of Drunkenness," *Penn. Med. J.,* **36**:190, 1932
14. Heise, H. A., "Alcohol and Automobile Accidents," *J. Am. Med. Assoc.,* **103**:739, 1934
15. Smith, S., and Stewart, C. P., "Diagnosis of Drunkenness from Excretion of Alcohol," *Brit. Med. J.,* **1**:87, 1932
16. Schmidt, M., "Alcohol Studies. II. Concentration of Alcohol in the Blood," *J. Ind. Hyg.,* **16**:355, 1934
17. Turner, R. G., "Blood Alcohol and Its Relation to Intoxication in Man," *Proc. Soc. Exp. Biol. and Med.,* **32**:1548, 1935

18. HOFFMANN, K., *Alkoholnachweis bei Verhehrsunfallen*, Berlin, Urban u. Schwarzenberg, 1937. Reviewed in *Brit. Med. J.*, **1**:535, 1937
19. JETTER, W. W., "Studies in Alcohol. I. The Diagnosis of Acute Alcoholic Intoxication by a Correlation of Clinical and Chemical Findings," *Am. J. Med. Sci.*, **196**:475, 1938
20. JETTER, W. W., "Studies in Alcohol. II. Experimental Feeding of Alcohol to Nonalcoholic Individuals," *Am. J. Med. Sci.*, **196**:487, 1938
21. HARGER, R. N., LAMB, E. B., and HULPIEU, H. R., "A Rapid Chemical Test for Intoxication Employing Breath," *J. Am. Med. Assoc.*, **110**:779, 1938
22. SELESNICK, S., "Alcoholic Intoxication: Its Diagnosis and Medicolegal Implications," *J. Am. Med. Assoc.*, **110**:775, 1938
23. MORGAN, H. W., "Scientific Tests for Intoxication," *J. Iowa State Med. Soc.*, **29**:53, 1939
24. LAUER, A. R., "The Effects of Alcohol on Driving," *J. Iowa State Med. Soc.*, **29**:282, 1939
25. BAVIS, D. F., "145 Drunken Drivers—Blood and Urine Alcohol Studies," *J. Lab. Clin. Med.*, **25**:823, 1940
26. NEWMAN, H. W., and FLETCHER, E., "The Effect of Alcohol on Driving Skill," *J. Am. Med. Assoc.*, **115**:1600, 1940
27. BERRY, D. S., "Alcohol as a Factor in Traffic Accidents," *Quart. J. Stud. Alcohol*, **1**:413, 1940
28. McGRATH, J., "The Method and Significance of Blood Alcohol Estimations," *Irish J. Med. Sci.*, 6th series, p. 304, 1939
29. CAMERON, A. T., "Alcohol and Automobile Driving," *Can. Med. Assoc. J.*, **43**:46, 1940
30. HAGGARD, H. W., GREENBERG, L. A., CARROLL, R. P., and MILLER, D. P., "The Use of Urine in the Chemical Test for Intoxication: Possible Errors and Their Avoidance," *J. Am. Med. Assoc.*, **115**:1680, 1940
31. HOLCOMB, R. L., "Alcohol in Relation to Traffic Accidents," *J. Am. Med. Assoc.*, **111**:1076, 1938
32. MIRSKY, I. A., PIKER, P., ROSENBAUM, M., and LEDERER, H., "'Adaptation' of the Central Nervous System to Varying Concentrations of Alcohol in the Blood," *Quart. J. Stud. Alcohol*, **2**:35, 1941
33. EGGLETON, M. G., "The Effect of Alcohol on the Central Nervous System," *Brit. J. Psychol.*, **32**:52, 1941

CHAPTER VI

TREATMENT OF ACUTE ALCOHOLIC INTOXICATION

It is the purpose of this chapter to evaluate the methods of treatment of central nervous system depression incidental to imbibition of alcohol. We shall thus confine the discussion to those measures directed at expediting removal of alcohol from the body or antagonizing its effect on the nervous system, leaving entirely out of account the treatment of alcoholism as a neuropsychiatric disease. In so doing, the problem is at once simplified and rendered of much less practical importance; for it is relatively rare that the acute toxicity of alcohol in itself is responsible for death. We have already noted the reasons for this, notably the onset of stupor, and emesis, which limits the intake of the drug. Nevertheless, deaths do occur directly attributable to the depressant effect of alcohol. Thus Jetter (1, 2) reported that of 1,000 individuals suspected of acute alcoholism and found to have alcohol in the blood, 2 died, with blood alcohol concentrations of 470 and 480 mg. %, while in another series of 800 suspects the only one to die had a blood alcohol concentration of 740 mg.%. In addition to the possibility of saving this relatively small number of acute alcoholics, any measure which will expedite recovery from alcoholic depression will undoubtedly prevent a much larger number of deaths due to complications of acute alcoholism, and is deserving of thorough investigation.

Mechanism of death.—In a consideration of possible therapeutic procedures, it is advantageous briefly to review our knowledge of the acute toxicity of alcohol. From the experimental work on animals it seems probable that death from acute alcoholism results from depression of the respiratory center in the medulla, with paralysis of respiration. This may be combated in several ways: the concentration of alcohol in the body may be reduced with more than normal rapidity by increasing either the rate of excretion or the rate of combustion of the alcohol; or the depressant action of alcohol on the respiratory center may be antagonized either by agents which stimulate the brain as a whole or the respiratory center specifically; or, finally, agents may be employed which may conceivably antagonize the depressant action of alcohol without actually being cerebral stimulants.

Increased excretion.—Let us first consider the possibility of increasing the rate of excretion of alcohol. It is assumed, of course, that any unabsorbed alcohol in the stomach has been removed by gastric lavage, so that the concentration in the blood is either at its maximum or more likely is on the decline when therapy is instituted. As was pointed out in a previous chapter, the two main excretory channels for alcohol are the urine and the breath. Since an immediate removal of alcohol is essential to effective therapy, diuretics to increase urinary output are not of practical value. This leaves the breath as the sole possibility. The only practicable method of increasing pulmonary ventilation is by inhalation of carbon dioxide, and this procedure has been made use of in practice. Hunter and Mudd (3) in 1924, on the suggestion of Yandell Henderson, administered carbon dioxide with an open-slot mask to a number of alcoholics. They had no idea of the actual carbon-dioxide concentration realized but stated that some evidence of the narcotic action of the gas was noted. Shivering due to increased heat loss was also noted, indicating the necessity of supplying heat to these patients. The effectiveness of the treatment was most marked in comatose patients. In order to demonstrate the removal of alcohol by the hyperventilation, which effected an increase in minute volume of 4 to 8 times the original values, they gave 28 cc. of 95% alcohol diluted to 150 cc. with fruit juice and water to a subject 3 hours after breakfast and took blood samples for analysis during the first 2¼ hours. On another day the same procedure was followed, but carbon dioxide was administered for two 25-minute periods, starting at 66 and 110 minutes after ingestion of the alcohol. On the day that carbon dioxide was given, the blood alcohol curve rose more rapidly to a higher maximum before the administration of the gas and subsequently fell more rapidly than on the control day. Since the period during which the blood studies were made was definitely the period of absorption, differences in absorption could well have produced the two curves without consideration of the possible effect of the gas. The conclusion that carbon-dioxide inhalation expedited removal of alcohol from the body to any appreciable extent was not, therefore, very well founded. This does not, however, in any way invalidate the reported beneficial effect on the course of the intoxication, which may, as we shall see, have a very different basis.

Robinson and Selesnick (4) revived the use of carbon-dioxide inhalations, employing a mixture of 90% oxygen and 10% carbon dioxide. They reported marked improvement clinically in a group of acute alcoholics, and presented figures showing very striking reductions in the venous blood alcohol concentration, reaching as high as 137 mg. % in a half-hour period, which they interpreted as indicating removal of a considerable amount of alcohol from the body. Newman and Card (5) took exception to the claim of removal of a significant amount of alcohol from the body by this degree of increased ventilation, and conducted an experimental investigation of the problem. To each of two human subjects they administered a dose of 2 cc. of alcohol per kilogram body weight intravenously, as a 20% solution in normal saline, the injection taking one hour. By this means the factor of absorption from the gastro-intestinal tract was eliminated. An hour was allowed to elapse for equilibration of alcohol between the blood and tissues, after which the first blood sample was taken. At the end of another hour a second blood sample was taken, the minute volume of respiration was determined with a spirometer, and inhalation of carbon dioxide 10% and oxygen 90% was begun without rebreathing. This was continued for 30 minutes, during which time the respiratory minute volume was twice determined and blood samples were taken. After the period of inhalation blood samples were again obtained at appropriate intervals. The curve of blood alcohol is seen in Figure 7. It will be noted that the rate of fall of the blood alcohol significantly increased during the period of inhalation, but on its discontinuance a rise occurred, followed by a period of slower fall, and finally by a slope comparable to that before inhalation.

To confirm these results with higher doses, giving concentrations comparable to those reported by Robinson and Seles-

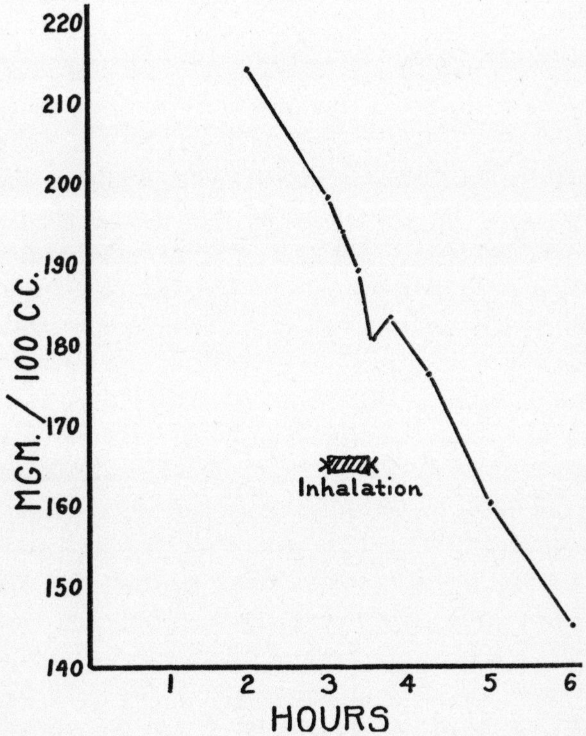

FIG. 7.—Blood alcohol concentration after intravenous injection of 2.0 cc. per kilogram in man, showing increased rate of fall during carbon-dioxide oxygen inhalation, with compensatory rise following.

nick, dogs were used and 4 cc. per kilogram were administered intravenously, producing a state of coma in all cases. In each case, inhalation of the gas mixture produced a more rapid fall, followed by a compensatory slowing of the fall of blood alcohol concentration. The significant fact obtained from this experimentation was that there was no actually significant change in the rate of decrease of total body alcohol brought about by the inhalation. True there was an acceleration of the decrease of venous blood alcohol during the inhalation period, to be accounted for by elimination of alcohol through the breath at a rate faster than could be made up for by diffusion of alcohol from the tissues into the blood, but after inhalation of the gases was stopped, this diffusion was responsible for the observed slow decline or even temporary rise of blood alcohol concentration. Since brain tissue has been shown to come rapidly into alcohol equilibrium with the blood, it is quite possible that there is also a transitory drop in brain alcohol concentration with carbon-dioxide inhalation, which may in part account for the clinical improvement noted, even though we must adhere to the dictum that no significant amount of alcohol is removed from the body as a whole by this procedure, a fact definitely in accord with theoretical considerations.

McFarland and Barach (6) investigated the effect of carbon-dioxide and oxygen inhalations on the blood alcohol concentration and performance of individuals given ¾ to 1¼ gm. of alcohol per kilogram orally. The blood alcohol concentration at the end of two hours was significantly lower when the gases were administered, except in about 20% of the cases, the same being true in regard to decrease in performance on the psychological tests. Since again the blood alcohol concentration was followed during the period of active absorption, no great reliance can be placed on these findings.

The evidence therefore seems to point to clinical improvement with inhalation of carbon dioxide and oxygen, without evidence adequately to support the view that this improvement is due to removal of a significant amount of alcohol from the body through the lungs. The transitory drop in blood alcohol, and probably consequently in brain alcohol concentration, may in part explain the clinical improvement. For the remainder, we shall see that carbon dioxide has a specific function in this regard.

Increased destruction.—Since it is so difficult for one to increase the removal of alcohol from the body by excretion, the possibility of increasing its rate of destruction in the body presents intriguing possibilities. In casting about for agents to accomplish this purpose, however, one must always bear in mind that alcohol is destroyed in the body by combustion and that for every gram of alcohol so destroyed approximately seven calories are produced. Since we know that the presence of alcohol in the body is not accompanied by any significant increase in total heat production, and yet may account for about half of the total basal energy requirement, it is at once obvious that we cannot expect to do more than double this rate of alcohol metabolism without running into serious difficulties in the matter of heat production. It has been demonstrated, as we have noted in the chapter on alcohol metabolism, that insulin in large doses is capable, both in man and in animals, of effecting approximately a 50% increase in the rate of alcohol metabolism. Carpenter (7) also felt he had demonstrated an increased rate of alcohol metabolism brought about by the administration of glucose in man. Goldfarb, Bowman, and Parker (8) have endeavored to utilize these effects in treating alcoholics. They found that the combination of 15 units of insulin given subcutaneously and 50 cc. of 50% glucose given intravenously was most effective, more than tripling the rate of fall of blood alcohol in severe cases of intoxication. In fact, they reported a fall of 275 mg. % in a period of two hours in one case. Since it requires approximately 150 gm. of alcohol to attain such a blood concentration, it is reasonable to assume that this reduction represents the burning of a like amount of alcohol, with production of 1,050 calories in two hours, or at a daily metabolic rate of 12,600 calories. We should certainly expect the production of a high fever by this metabolic rate, no indication of which is presented by the authors. The alternatives remain that the alcohol is not actually completely burned but rather is stored in another form, for which there is no evidence in the literature, or that the figures are unreliable. Certainly they are far out of line with any reported from controlled animal experimentation with even much greater doses of insulin and glucose. Wortis, Bowman, and Goldfarb (9) further reported the efficacy of insulin and glucose in treating "toxic alcoholics" with little or no alcohol in their blood. Taylor and Cross (10) reported treatment of one case with glucose and insulin—a pickaninny who ingested 200 cc. of 70% rubbing alcohol, with a blood alcohol 4 hours later of 384 mg.%. Treatment was not started until 12 hours after ingestion, at a time when the blood alcohol concentration must already have fallen considerably; so in spite of the fact that the patient first became responsive right after the insulin was injected, there is little to indicate that the treatment played a major part in the recovery.

The synergistic action of glucose and insulin in accelerating alcohol metabolism is not subscribed to by Bickel (11), who reported that while either insulin or sugar was effective in increasing the rate of decline of blood alcohol concentration, when insulin was given with sugar the increased rate of fall of blood alcohol usually seen with insulin alone was not present. He also stated that while insulin improved the condition of intoxicated subjects, high blood sugar concentration prevented this. It is not possible to reconcile these findings with those mentioned above. We may state, however, that certainly insulin and possibly also glucose are effective in accelerating the rate of alcohol disappearance. In controlled studies in animals and man the increase in rate does not exceed 50%, which probably would not be of significant help in cases of acute alcoholism. That the beneficial clinical effect may be due not to increased rate of metabolism at all, but rather to a specific effect of glucose, is indicated by work we will present later in this chapter.

Pharmacologic antagonists.—It is thus seen that because of the small percentage of alcohol that is excreted, even a considerable increase of elimination by the excretory channels does not significantly expedite removal of alcohol from the body, and that because the destruction of alcohol in the body is an oxidative process and already accounts for a large percentage of the heat requirement this process cannot be speeded up sufficiently to reduce dangerous concentrations of alcohol quickly. There remain for consideration those measures aimed at increasing the efficiency of neural function in the face of high alcohol concentrations. A number of such pharmacologic antagonists have been investigated in recent years. We have already mentioned the work of Goldfarb, Bowman, and Parker (8), who used intravenous injections of glucose in conjunction with insulin in an endeavor to remove alcohol more rapidly by oxidation, and reported excellent clinical results. These results may at least in part be explained by the findings of Haggard and Greenberg (12), who investigated the effect of blood sugar concentration on the lethal concentration of alcohol in the jugular blood of rats receiving repeated intraperitoneal injections of alcohol. They found that with a normal blood sugar concentration around 100 mg.% the lethal concentration of alcohol in the jugular blood was 930 mg.%. When the blood sugar was reduced to 70 mg.% by prolonged fasting, this lethal concentration was reduced to 800 mg.%; and the amount of alcohol administered to achieve this concentration was 6.5 gm. per kilogram, as contrasted with 7.75 gm. per kilogram with normal blood sugar. When, on the other hand, blood sugar was increased to 200 mg.% by forcing sugar, the lethal concentration was increased to 1,200 mg.% and the dose to 11.0 gm. per kilogram. This work is of the utmost importance if confirmed, as it indicates a very simple method of significantly increasing the tolerance to lethal doses of alcohol.

Oxygen.—Because of the similarity of symptomatology of acute alcoholic intoxication and oxygen deprivation, Barach (13) investigated the effect of increased oxygen tension on intoxication. He found that while nonalcoholic rabbits could withstand an oxygen tension as low as 9%, rabbits given 3 to 4 cc. of alcohol fell down in coma at the same oxygen tension. This is hardly more than a demonstration of the effect of the summation of two toxic effects, and in no way proves a similarity of the two toxic agents. Nor did the recovery of the alcoholic rabbits when oxygen tension was increased in any way alter this conclusion. This is further borne out by the fact that lethal doses of alcohol killed as many rabbits at oxygen concentrations of from 50 to 90% as they did in air. The author therefore logically concluded that intoxication produced by alcohol is not due to the type of oxygen lack capable of relief by oxygen inhalation. This is supported by the work of Haggard and coworkers (14), who found the lethal concentration of alcohol in the jugular blood of rats given alcohol by repeated intraperitoneal injection to be 930 mg.% in air and 929 mg.% in an atmosphere of oxygen. From this they very reasonably concluded that oxygen was ineffective in combating acute alcoholism. It is equally doubtful if the effect of alcohol noted in situations in which the oxygen concentration is subject to criticism, notably at poker parties, may be attributable to oxygen deficiency. Just what factors are in operation to vary the effect of a given concentration of alcohol in the blood, whether in a cool, crisp temperature in the open air or in the tobacco-laden atmosphere of the gambling room, remains to be elucidated. Nor can we expect to receive the answer from sources in any way suspect of partisanship.

Strychnine.—A possible pharmacologic antidote to alcohol was strychnine, which has long been known to lower synaptic resistance. Gold and Travell (15) showed conclusively that alcohol administered intravenously to dogs, rabbits, cats, and frogs was an effective antidote in strychnine poisoning, protecting against at least five minimal lethal doses, and with care in timing the injection as much as ten M.L.D. From this investigation, they went on to a study of the effect of strychnine on poisoning by alcohol. They found that, contrary to expectations, even large doses of strychnine were ineffective in protecting against lethal doses of alcohol. True, in animals profoundly depressed by alcohol, large doses of strychnine did somewhat antagonize the effects of alcohol on the higher centers, so that, instead of complete paralysis, motion was possible; but this was evident only when the dosage was pushed to the point where reflex hyperexcitability or convulsions ensued. Nor did strychnine have any effect on the rate of recovery from alcohol narcosis. We can thus dismiss this agent as of no value in the treatment of acute alcoholism.

Barbiturates.—Carriere, Huriez, and Willoquet (17) reported an antagonism between a barbiturate and alcohol. They found that repeated injections of alcohol by the intravenous route protected rabbits from fatal doses of gardenal. This work is directly contradicted by the carefully controlled experiments of Dille and Ahlquist (18), who demonstrated unequivocally that instead of antagonism between alcohol and barbital there was a marked potentiated synergism so far as the narcotic effect was concerned. That this does not apply to lethal doses of alcohol is indicated by the work of Haggard *et al.* (14), who found no change in the lethal concentration of alcohol in the jugular blood of rats on administration of 5 to 50 mg. per kilogram of amytal. At any rate, it is apparent that the barbiturates are not indicated in the treatment of acute alcoholic intoxication.

Benzedrine.—Benzedrine sulphate in a dose of 3 mg. per kilogram was found by Haggard and his coworkers (14) to be ineffective in changing the lethal jugular blood alcohol concentration in rats. Reifenstein (19), however, found that individuals in alcoholic stupor roused in about 30 minutes after administration of 10 to 30 mg. of benzedrine intravenously. An oral dose of 5 to 10 mg. was found effective against the "hangover." The same author later (20), working with the rabbit, came to the conclusion that while benzedrine acted as an analeptic against narcotic doses of alcohol, it was ineffective in protecting against lethal doses. On the other hand, alcohol protected against 1½ to 2 lethal doses of benzedrine. Thus we may say that while benzedrine in therapeutic doses may be effective in hastening the sobering-up process, it is not capable of combating the severe depression responsible for death from acute alcoholism.

Carbon dioxide.—It has been fairly conclusively demonstrated by Haggard and his coworkers (14) that acute deaths from alcohol poisoning are due to depression of the respiratory center in the medulla, and that the concentration of alcohol effective in producing this paralysis is quite constant when other factors are not changed. We have already seen that the lethal concentration is influenced by blood sugar concentration, while it is not changed by increasing the environmental oxygen tension. When, however, the carbon-dioxide tension is increased to 10%, the minimal lethal concentration rises from 930 mg.% to 1,030 mg.%. This effect is no doubt due to stimulation of the respiratory center by the carbon dioxide, which is the physiological stimulant for that center, so antagonizing the depressant action of the alcohol; and it is very likely that this action, rather than any decrease in total body alcohol, is the reason for the clinical improvement noted by Hunter and Mudd (3) and Robinson and Selesnick (4) when alcoholics were treated with carbon-dioxide inhalations. There can be no doubt that such inhalations may at times be of distinct value in treating respiratory depression due to acute alcoholic intoxication.

Metrazol.—Orenstein, Bowman, Kagan, and Goldfarb (21) have employed metrazol in the treatment of acute alcoholism. Two groups of patients, one violent and the other comatose, were treated, 5 cc. of metrazol being given intravenously in 30 seconds without the production of convulsions. This suggests that at least alcohol antagonizes the convulsive action of metrazol.

They reported that excited alcoholics quieted down in from 2 to 10 minutes, while many comatose patients regained consciousness in from 5 to 30 minutes. There was no notable change in blood alcohol concentration to account for these results. The biphasic effect was explained in the following manner: metrazol produced cortical stimulation; this increased cortical inhibition in the excited patients and thus quieted them, while the depressed cortical function of the depressed patients was stimulated and they aroused. In view of this ambivalence of effect, it would seem that confirmatory investigation was indicated.

McCrea and Taylor (22) have used metrazol in experimental alcoholic intoxication in dogs. They administered 3.0 to 7.2 cc. of absolute alcohol per kilogram as a 20% solution intravenously to a series of animals, until respiration was arrested. Artificial respiration was tried for from 4 to 10 minutes, and if spontaneous respiration did not then take place metrazol 4.4 to 7.0 mg. per kilogram was given intravenously. In all cases respiration started spontaneously after this procedure in a few seconds. There was no arousal from coma with the 7.0 cc. per kilogram dose; but with the 3.5 to 5.0 cc. doses there was arousal for a period of 30 to 45 minutes, consisting of an ability of the dogs to rise on the forelegs and yap, but no more. Following this period coma again supervened. The rate of disappearance of alcohol from the blood was in no way affected. This work seems to substantiate the clinical investigation of Orenstein *et al.* (21), and indicates further clinical trial in selected cases, always bearing in mind the potentially convulsive nature of the drug.

Measures of clinical value.—In reviewing the therapeutic armamentarium against acute alcoholic intoxication, one is struck by the few procedures which give promise of clinical value and the little work upon which their use rests. The latter fact is probably due to the infrequency with which the physician meets the necessity of treating dangerous depression from alcohol. Certainly so long as there is not marked depression of respiration, the wisest course to follow is one of watchful expectancy, with measures directed at maintaining body temperature and a free air-way, after of course removing any unabsorbed alcohol from the stomach. When respiratory failure threatens, inhalation of carbon dioxide 10%, without rebreathing, is definitely indicated; and, if a good response is not obtained, metrazol in subconvulsant doses intravenously should be tried. Also, it would seem advisable to give glucose intravenously, with or without doses of insulin not to exceed 15 units hypodermically. The objective should be not so much to try to sober the individual up rapidly as to tide over a crisis of respiratory depression, which constitutes the real danger to life of acute alcoholic intoxication.

REFERENCES

1. Jetter, W. W., "Chemical and Clinical Diagnosis of Acute Alcoholism," *New Engl. J. Med.*, **221**:1019, 1939
2. Jetter, W. W., "Studies in Alcohol. I. The Diagnosis of Acute Alcoholic Intoxication by a Correlation of Clinical and Chemical Findings," *Am. J. Med. Sci.*, **196**:475, 1938
3. Hunter, F. T., and Mudd, S. G., "Carbon Dioxide Treatment in Acute Alcoholic Intoxication," *Boston Med. Surg. J.*, **190**:971, 1924
4. Robinson, L. J., and Selesnick, S., "The Treatment of Acute Alcoholism with 10% CO_2 and 90% O_2 Inhalation," *J. Am. Med. Assoc.*, **105**:1734, 1935
5. Newman, H. W., and Card, J., "The Actual Value of Carbon Dioxide–Oxygen Inhalation in Accelerating the Reduction of Total Body Alcohol," *J. Am. Med. Assoc.*, **106**:595, 1936
6. McFarland, R. A., and Barach, A. L., "The Relationship between Alcoholic Intoxication and Anoxemia," *Am. J. Med. Sci.*, **192**:186, 1936
7. Carpenter, T. M., "The Effect of Glucose on the Metabolism of Ethyl Alcohol in Man," *J. Pharmacol.*, **60**:264, 1937
8. Goldfarb, W., Bowman, K. M., and Parker, S., "The Treatment of Acute Alcoholism with Glucose and Insulin," *J. Clin. Investigation*, **18**:581, 1939
9. Wortis, J., Bowman, K. M., and Goldfarb, W., "The Use of Insulin in the Treatment of Alcoholism," *Med. Clin. North America*, **24**:671, 1940
10. Taylor, H. M., and Cross, A. R., "Treatment of Acute Alcoholism with Insulin," *J. Pediat.*, **16**:341, 1940
11. Bickel, A., "The Biologic Effect of Alcohol on Metabolism," quoted in "Foreign Letters, Berlin," *J. Am. Med. Assoc.*, **106**:2171, 1936

12. Haggard, H. W., and Greenberg, L. A., "The Effects of Alcohol as Influenced by Blood Sugar," *Science*, **85**:608, 1937
13. Barach, A. L., "Action of Oxygen in Counteracting Intoxication," *Am. J. Physiol.*, **107**:610, 1934
14. Haggard, H. W., Greenberg, L. A., Rakieten, N., and Cohen, L. H., "Studies in the Absorption, Distribution, and Elimination of Alcohol. VII," *J. Pharmacol.*, **69**:266, 1940
15. Gold, H., and Travell, J., "Ethyl Alcohol and Strychnine Antagonism," *J. Pharmacol.*, **52**:30, 1934
16. Gold, H., and Travell, J., "Strychnine in Poisoning by Alcohol," *J. Pharmacol.*, **52**:345, 1934
17. Carriere, G., Huriez, C., and Willoquet, P., "Étude experimentale des injections intraveineuses d'alcool au cours d'intoxications par le gardenal," *Compt. rend. soc. biol.*, **116**:188, 1934
18. Dille, J. L., and Ahlquist, R. R., "The Synergism of Ethyl Alcohol and Sodium Pentobarbital," *J. Pharmacol.*, **61**:385, 1937
19. Reifenstein, E. C., and Davidoff, E., "The Treatment of Alcoholic Psychoses with Benzedrine Sulphate," *J. Am. Med. Assoc.*, **110**:1811, 1938
20. Reifenstein, E. C., "Amphetamine Sulphate Ethyl Alcohol Antagonism in the Rabbit," *J. Pharmacol.*, **69**:298, 1940
21. Orenstein, L. L., Bowman, K. M., Kagan, J. R., and Goldfarb, W., "Use of Metrazol in Treatment of Acute Alcoholism," *Am. J. Psychiatry*, **96**:589, 1939
22. McCrea, F. D., and Taylor, H. M., "The Use of Pentamethylenetetrazol (Metrazol) as a Respiratory Stimulant in Acute Alcoholic Depression," *J. Pharmacol.*, **68**:41, 1940

AUTHOR INDEX

SUBJECT INDEX